WARSAW

AND SURROUNDINGS

PHOTOGRAPHY: STANISŁAWA, JOLANTA AND RAFAŁ JABŁOŃSKI
TEKST: RAFAŁ JABŁOŃSKI

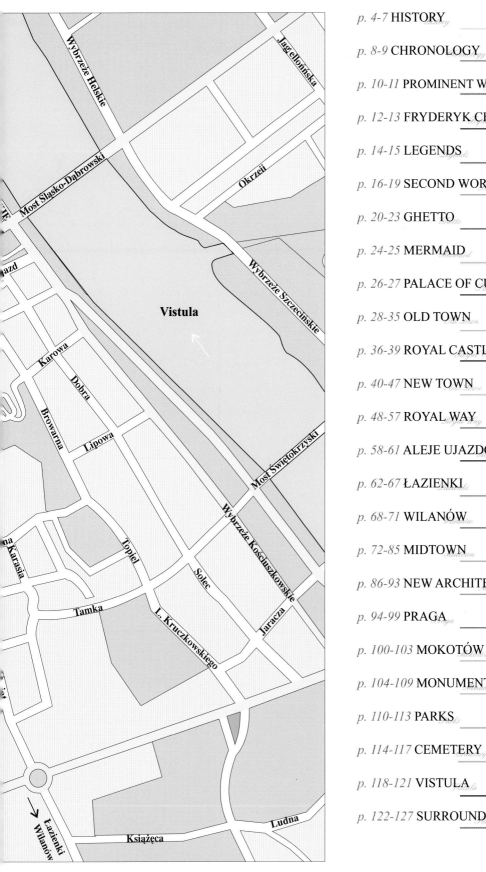

HISTORY

Warsaw, Europe's youngest capital, is a city with a long history. Already in the 10th century, in the region of today's right-bank Bródno district there existed a fortified-town complex. In the centuries that followed, the settlements of Kamion, Targowe Wielkie and Solec developed. The latter was protected by a fortified castle town known as Jazdów and situated on the site of today's Botanical Gardens. Destroyed by invading Lithuanian Jadvingian barbarians, it was rebuilt at a different, more defensible site. Bolesław II, the Duke of Masovia, probably chose the site because of its tall escarpment and superior water supply from the Rivers Drna and Bełczącej (now the East-West Thoroughfare). The town was named Warszawa (Warszowa) from the name Warsz that was frequently encountered in the Rawicz-Niedźwiadek clan which owned the nearby village of Solec. In time, a powerful castle was erected at that site, and the town began developing to the south of it and was walled in. The then popular chessboard layout with a central market-place was used. St John's Church was built, a wójt (local administrator) was chosen and a Town Council deliberated in the town hall erected in the late 14th and early 15th centuries.

Duke Janusz I the Elder resolved to make Warsaw the capital of the Duchy of Masovia. Important ducal assemblies began taking place and the earthly remains of successive Masovian rulers were laid to rest in St John's Church. At the start of the 14th century, beyond the New Town Gate. a new commercial settlement known as New Town began emerging. A marketplace with a town hall was also laid out, and the district's commercial character was attested to by its numerous granaries, storehouses and workshops. Defensive walls were not erected, however.

Warsaw's further development was affected by the rise of jurisdictions. Those were private aristocrat-owned towns not

1. View of Warsaw according to a copper engraving in a 1662 book by S. Stawicki.

subject to the municipal authorities. They had their own administration, and some of them also had their own marketplace and town hall. They survived till the end of the 18th century.

Warsaw's central location gained in importance as the borders of the Royal Republic and subsequently - after the

2. Warsaw panorama according to Dahlberg, 1656.

3. Warsaw Panorama seen from the Vistula, wood-cut from the "Constitution of the General Assembly of AD 1589".

Polish-Lithuanian union - the Commonwealth of Two Nations expanded. It was there that the important transport routes converged and, from 1569, national General Crown Assemblies took place. Representatives of the aristocracy and gentry would come to such assemblies from every corner of the land. From 1573, elections of Polish kings were held in the fields of Wola. The third successive electoral assembly elected Swedish-born Zygmunt III Vasa as king. Following the fire at Kraków's Wawel Castle in 1596, the king decided to move the capital from Kraków to Warsaw. Apart from considerations of state, the king's decision was influenced by his nostalgia for his homeland, so remote from Kraków. Warsaw became the country's political and economic centre. Aristocrats, noblemen, artists and traders would gather at the court for which the castle was renovated. As more and more people flocked to the town, it began to grow and make room for new palaces and dwelling-houses.

During the reigns of the Saxon Dynasty (King August II and III) a short-lived construction boom occurred. Work was conducted at the Royal Castle where new chambers were created, headed by the impressive Deputies' Chamber. It was there on 3 May 1791 that Europe's first democratic constitutions was adopted.

Warsaw entered a period of dynamic development during the reign of Poland's last king, Stanisław August Poniatowski. The best architects renovated the Royal Castle, and the old Lubomirski bathhouses was transformed into the king's summer residence.

The period of Poland's partitions, which lasted with interruptions for 120 years, reduced Warsaw to the rank of a provincial town. Armed uprisings such as the Kościuszko Insurrection, the November Insurrection and January In-

4. Assembling the King Sigismund III column, a drawing by Hondius.

5. Map of Warsaw and Praga from 1705.

surrection only increased the reprisals on the part of the occupying powers.

Total renewal came only when Poland regained its independence in 1918. New districts -Żoliborz, Bielany and Saska Kępa - were developed. An airport was built in Okęcie.

The year 1939 augured Warsaw's further destruction. Already on 1 September, its inhabitants were subjected to a German bombardment in which the Royal Castle caught fire. Warsaw's total destruction occurred in 1944. After the

6. Warsaw emblem of 1659.

7. View of Warsaw, 18th-century engraving by Bernardo Bellotto-Canaletto.

8. Baryczek Panorama of Warsaw from c. 1755-79.

63-day Warsaw Uprising, the Germans systematically looted and set fire to the city.

Immediately after the war ended, the people of Warsaw set about raising their city from the rubble. Old Town as well as most palaces and historic dwelling-houses were rebuilt.

But the true development of Warsaw began only after 1989 in the Third Republic. The restoration of democracy and a market economy enabled its inhabitants to make up for the time they lost during the communist period. The encroachment of modernity can be seen at every turn.

9. View of the Old Town Marketplace in 1900.

CHRONOLOGY

700-400 BC – A burial ground associated with the Lusatian culture had existed on the site of today's Grochów.

10th century AD – A castle-town existed in Bródno.

1065 – Boleslaus the Bold grants the settlement of Kamion in Mogilno to the Benedictine Order

1262 – A Lithuanian-Jadvingian attack is launched against Jazdów (now Ujazdów).

1281 – The duke of Płock Boleslaus II launches an attack on Jazdów.

1289 – The oldest known Warsaw chronicle, which mentions the foundation of St George's Church, is recorded.

1408 – New Warsaw is established to the north of the defensive walls of today's New Town.

1413 – The capital of Masovia is moved from Czersk to Warsaw.

1526 – the duchy of Masovia becomes part of the Kingdom of Poland following the death of the last duke of Masovia.

1529 – The first General Sejm (parliamentary assembly) is held in Warsaw.

1569 – Warsaw is proclaimed the permanent venue of General Sejm assemblies of the Kingdom of Poland and Lithuania following the Union of Brześć.

1569-74 – The first permanent bridge across the Vistula is built.

1573 – As a result of the first free royal election in Warsaw, Frenchman Henri de Valois is elected king of Poland.

1578 – King Stefan Batory accepts the allegiance of his fief, Prussian Duke Georg Friedrich.

1596 – Warsaw is proclaimed the capital of Poland, marking a major turning point in the city's history. King Sigismund III moves his seat from Kraków to Warsaw.

1606-07 – Warsaw's first water mains are built at Nalewki street.

1611 – Hetman Stefan Żółkiewski makes a triumphal entrance into Warsaw following his victorious war against Muscovy, leading Tsar Vasil Suysky and his two brothers as captives.

1621 – Military fortifications known as Sigismund's Ramparts encircle Warsaw.

1624 – Warsaw struggles with the plague for eight months.

1638-43 – The Arsenal of the Commonwealth is built.

1644 – The King Sigismund III Vasa monument is erected by his son.

1648 – King Ladislaus IV Vasa grants municipal rights to Praga on the right bank of the Vistula.

1655-58 – Warsaw is thrice captured by Swedish and Hungarian troops during the 'Deluge'. The city was burnt and

10. Zamkowy Square. M. Zalewski.

11. The ruins of the Old Town in 1945.

plundered, and its population dropped from 15,000 to 2,000.

1666 – Tytus Liwiusz Burattini sets up the first astronomical observatory at Ujazdów.

1670 – The first permanent post office goes into service at Krzywe Koło street.

1677-92 – Wilanów Palace is built for King John III Sobieski.

1695 – The Marywil trading and service complex is built.

1713-30 – The Saxon Axis, a 1.5-kilometre urban-development scheme, linked to the construction of a royal residence for Augustus III of Saxony, is laid out.

1740 – Stanisław Konarski establishes his Collegium Nobilium, the first school of higher education.

1740 – A Paving Commission, headed by Marshal Franciszek Bielński, is set up to improve the city's sanitary conditions. (Warsaw's High street, ulica Marszałkowska, was named in his honour).

1747 – The first public library is opened at the initiative of the Brothers Załuski.

1748 – The first permanent theatre, known as Operalnia, is opened at the behest of Augustus II.

1764 – The coronation of Stanislaus Augustus Poniatowski, the first outside of Kraków, is held at Warsaw Cathedral.

1765 – The Commission of Good Order is established.

1765 –The first permanent public stage is opened at the National Theatre.

1765 – Stanislaus Augustus Poniatowski establishes the Knights' School, one of whose students is Tadeusz Kościuszko.

1766-95 – The Łazienki palace and park complex is conceived.

1772 – The first street lamps and permanently named streets appear.

1773 – The Sejm establishes the Commission of National Education, Europe's first public education ministry.

1788 – The Great Sejm, which would remain in session until 1792, begins its deliberations. Its goal was the rebuild Poland's collapsing statehood.

1790 – Powązki Cemetery, Warsaw's first municipal necropolis, is established.

1791 – Praga becomes part of Warsaw.

1794 – Warsaw Insurrection is the name given to a rebellion against the Russian garrison during the Kościuszko Insurrection. Cobbler Jan Kiliński represents the townspeople.

1795-1806 – The city is occupied by Prussian troops.

1800 – Stanisław Staszic sets up the Warsaw Society of Friends of Learning.

1806 – Napoleon's troops enter the city.

1807 – The Duchy of Warsaw with its capital in Warsaw is established as a Polish state subordinated to Napoleon.

1815 – The Duchy of Warsaw is transformed into the Congress Kingdom forming part of the Russian Empire.

1816 – Warsaw university is founded.

1828 – The Bank of Poland is created.

1830-31 – The November Insurrection against Russia is caused by restrictions on national liberties.

1825-33 – The Wielki Theatre is built.

1834 – A permanent fire brigade is created.

1840-48 – The first railway linking the city with Vienna is built.

1863-64 – The January Insurrection, a national-liberation uprising against the Russian occupation forces, is waged.

1864 – The first permanent bridge across the Vistula goes into service.

1906 – The first electric trams appear.

1915-18 – German occupation during the First World War.

1918 – Warsaw becomes the capital of the reborn Polish State, the Second Republic of Poland.

1920 – Known as the 'Miracle of the Vistula', the Battle of Warsaw during the Polish-Bolshevik War is acknowledged as one of the decisive battles in world history, which stopped Soviet communism's march on the West.

1930 – Okęcie Airport is opened.

1st September 1939 – The first German bombs launching World War Two fall on the city.

28th September 1939 – The capital capitulates to Nazi forces.

15th November 1940 – The German occupation forces set up a Warsaw Ghetto surrounded by a wall.

19th April – 16th May 1943 – Uprising in the Warsaw Ghetto, triggered by the extermination of the Jewish population.

1st August – 2nd October 1944 – 63-day Warsaw Uprising against the German occupation. 150,000 civilians and 10,000 insurgents perished. The city was 25 percent destroyed.

17th January 1945 – Soviet and Polish troops march into the city.

1953 – Reconstruction of the Old Town.

1955 – Construction of the Palace of Culture and Science, 'a gift of the Soviet people to Warsaw'.

1971-74 – Reconstruction of the Royal Castle.

1991 – Opening of the Warsaw Stock Exchange.

1995 – Opening of the metro.

PROMINENT WARSOVIANS

Józef Piłsudski (1867–1935)

Independence activist, politician, statesman and first Marshal of Poland. The architect of Poland's independent statehood in 1918, he became Interim Chief of State. He was commander-in-chief of Poland's Armed Forces during the Polish-Soviet War of 1920 and the author of the battle plan pf the Battle of Warsaw, known as 'the Miracle of the Vistula'. Fought on 12-25 August 1920 between Polish forces and the Soviet Army under General Tukhachevsky, it has been acknowledged as one of the decisive battles in world history. It enabled Poland to maintain its hard-won independence and stopped the expansion of the communist revolution to Western Europe. Piłsudski had advocated an Inter-Sea Confederation comprising the lands of the former Polish-Lithuanian Commonwealth. But it was his opponent Roman Dmowski's concept of a more compact national state that won out. In view of the political crisis engulfing Poland, Piłsudski decided on a military coup carried out on 12-14 May 1926 with the support of a majroity of Poles.

12. Józef Piłsudski.

13. Jan Kiliński.

Jan Kiliński (1760–1819)

A cobbler by trade, during the 1794 Kościuszko Insurrection against Russian occupation he led the townspeople of Warsaw into battle. He was the only representative of the middle burgher class appointed by the king to membership of the Provisional Substitute Council which assumed power in Warsaw during the insurrection. For his service, he was nominated a colonel by Tadeusz Kościuszko. Arrested by the Prussians and handed over to the Russians, Kiliński was exiled into the depths of Russian. Upon his return he wrote memoirs.

Maria Skłodowska-Curie (1867–1934)

Born in Warsaw at Freta Street 16, this outstanding chemist and physicist spent most of her life in France. There she studied and pursued her scientific career. Among her main achievements was her theory of radiation and the discovery of two new elements: Radium and Polonium. She also conducted research on the use of radiation therapy in the treatment of cancer. She was twice awarded the Nobel Prize: in 1903 with her husband Pierre in Physics and in 1911 in Chemistry.

Henryk Sienkiewicz (1846-1916)

A novelist and journalist of the positivist period, he ranked amongst the world's most popular writers, whose works were translated into many different languages including Arabic and Japanese. His favourite literary form was the historical novel. In Poland, the greatest popularity was enjoyedbyhis"Trilogy" comprising "With Fire and Sword", "Pan Wołodyjowski"and "The Deluge". His novel "Quo Vadis" gained the greatest popularity abroad. His novels "Knights of the Cross" and 'In Desert and Wilderness' also won a considerable following. In 1905, he was awarded the Nobel Literary Prize for his overall literary achievements. In 1900, Sienkiewicz received a manor house in Oblęgorek near Kielce as a gift from the Polish nation.

Isaac Bashevis Singer (1904-91)

A well-known writer of Jewish ancestry, he wrote in Yiddish. For quite some time, he had lived at Krochmalna street in Warsaw and had his writings printed in the Warsaw journal "Literarisze Bleter". In 1936, he emigrated to the United States. In 1978, he was awarded the Nobel Prize for Literature. His works include the novel 'The Magician of Lublin'.

15. Ignacy Padarewski monument in the Ujazdowski Park.

14. Maria Curie-Skłodowska.

Jan Kiepura (1902-66)

A popular singer (tenor) and actor, he began his artistic career on the stage of the Warsaw Opera and gained his first international exposure in Vienna. He performed at the world's most prestigious venues including La Scala, Covent Garden and the Metropolitan Opera. He was also known as a silver-screen star appearing in numerous films produced by Hollywood and German studios.

Ignacy Paderewski (1860-1941)

An outstanding pianist, composer, politician and independence activist, he studied music at the Warsaw Institute of Music and launched his solo career at the Warsaw Philharmonic. He achieved international renown performing abroad in such countries as France and the United States. He also was involved in diplomatic efforts on behalf of Poland's independence. After Poland and regained its independence, he returned to Poland where in 1919 he became the prime minister and foreign minister.

Czesław Miłosz (1911-2004)

A poet, prose writer, essayist and literary historian, he spent nearly the entire World War Two period in Warsaw. In 1951, he emigrated to France and later to the USA. W 1980 he was awarded the Nobel Literary Prize for his life's achievements. As a poet, he was ranked within the catastrophic stream of what was known as the second avant-garde. His poetry was banned in communist Poland and appeared in the underground. Aside from extensive poetry, he also produced prose works (including "The Captive Mind" and "Issa Valley") and did translations.

FRYDERYK CHOPIN

16. *Fryderyk Chopin.*

17. *Epitaph containing the heart of Fryderyk Chopin enshrined at Warsaw's Holy Cross Church.*

Fryderyk Chopin (1810-49) - the outstanding, world-renowned composer and pianist was born at Żelazowa Wola near Łowicz to the family of Mikołaj Chopin, a Frenchman from Lorraine, and Polish noblewoman, Justyna Krzyżanowska. Chopin's father was employed at Żelazowa Wola as the home tutor of Count Fryderyk Skarbek, the proprietor of the local estate. The Chopin family lived in one of the annexes of the no longer existing Żelazowa Wola manor house. Both of Fryderyk's parents were musically inclined: his father played the violin and flute and his mother - the piano.

Already in autumn 1810, the Chopin family moved to Warsaw. There Fryderyk took piano lessons, at first with his mother and later with Wojciech Żywny, a Czech.

There Chopin first tried his hand at composition at the age of seven, and two polonaises-in G Minor and B Major-were the result. At the age of eight, Fryderyk gave his first public performance to the delight of Warsaw's salons, where he became a sought-after attraction. When he turned 15, his first two mazurkas-in G Major and Rondo in C Minor-appeared in print. In 1826-29, Chopin developed his talent at the Main School of Music under the tutelage of Józef Elsner. Exempted from having to take further piano lessons owing to this unique playing style, he studied composition and harmony. Following a short sojourn in Vienna, he travelled to Paris, where he settled permanently. Bid farewell by his friends at the outskirts of Warsaw, he was given an urn containing Polish soil which would later be sprinkled on his grave. He would never see his native land again. In Paris, he lived the life of a virtuoso, admired by the local elite. He performed concerts, composed and gave piano lessons. There he met the well-known writer Aurora Dudevant using the pseudonym George Sand, with whom he was romantically involved for several years. Together they travelled to Spanish Majorca to nurse the ailing Fryderyk back to health. Chopin was suffering from tuberculosis, but for quite some time his doctors had dismissed his ailment as

18. *Chopin Museum at Warsaw's Gniński-Ostrogski Palace.*

19. Chopin manor house in Żelazowa Wola. The composer's birthplace.

20. Fryderyk Chopin monument in Warsaw's Łazienki Park.

a non-threatening sore throat. Unfortunately, the composer's health continued to deteriorate, and he composed and performed less and less. In 1848, he travelled to London and Scotland. In London, he gave his last concert to benefit Polish émigrés. He died in Paris in 1849.

Chopin had already been regarded as a musical genius as both a composer and virtuoso by his contemporaries. His compositions were able to extract from the piano a dynamic, hitherto unencountered potential, producing rich, undreamt of world of sounds. His innovations in the realm of harmony enabled his compositions to speak a completely new and surprisingly rich musical language. The balance and perfection of his works endowed them with a touch of classical styles, whilst their poetry and moodiness rank his music within the romantic convention then in vogue. The romantic trait of his compositions was their folk, and hence national component. As Karol Szymanowski once said, in his Mazurkas and Polonaises Chopin wanted to 'take the eternally beating heart of the race in his hands and re-create it in the form of a perfect, universally comprehensible work of art.'

21. Church at Brochów, where Fryderyk Chopin was baptised.

WARSAW LEGENDS

WARS AND SAWA

Long, long ago, on the banks of the Vistula stood a tiny hut inhabited by the fisherman Wars and his wife Sawa. One day, the local lord Ziemiomysł was hunting in the vicinity. In pursuit of game, he had wandered away from his party and lost his way in the forest. Evening was already approaching when he reached the banks of the Vistula and spotted the hut of Wars and Sawa. Since wandering in the forest at night was dangerous, the prince knocked on the door and requested shelter. Wars and Sawa lavished their hospitality upon him, fed him and offered him a place to stay – an offer that was gratefully accepted. The next morning, the prince thanked the poor fisherfolk for their help and was said to have told them: "You did not hesitate to receive a stranger under your roof and rescued him from hunger, cold and perhaps even from wild beasts. Therefore these lands will for ever more be known as Warszowa, so your kindness shall not be forgotten".

22. Warsaw Mermaid monument at the Wybrzeże Kościusz-kowskie riverside.

THE MERMAID

It was ages ago that two mermaid sisters, beautiful women with fish tails who had lived in the depths of the sea, swam into the Baltic from the Atlantic. One of them took a fancy to the cliffs of the Straits of Denmark, and to this day she may be seen sitting on a rock at the entrance to the Port of Copenhagen.

The other mermaid swam to Gdańsk, a great Baltic port, and then travelled down the Vistula. According to legend, she left the water at the foot of today's New Town, more or less where her statue now stands, and rested on the sandy riverbank. Since the area appealed to her, she decided to stay. Local fishermen soon noticed that someone was stirring up the waters of the Vistula, knotting up their nets and releasing the fish they had caught. But since they were charmed by the mermaid's singing, they did nothing about it.

A wealthy merchant once saw the mermaid and her splendid singing. He calculated how much he would earn if he captured the mermaid and began showing her at fairs. He deceptively captured the mermaid and locked her in a wooden shed with no access to water. The mermaid's plaintive cries were heard by a young farmhand, a fisherman's son and together with a group of friends freed her under the cover of night. In gratitude, the mermaid told the townsfolk they could always count on her in times of need. That is why the Warsaw mermaid is armed with a sword and shield – to defend the town.

BASILISK

Long, long ago, in the cellar of a house at Krzywe Koło Street there lived a ferocious monster known as the Basilisk, who had hatched from an egg laid by a seven-year-old cock and bred by a poisonous viper.

He had the head of a cock and the body of a spiny serpent. The dungeon watched over by the Basilisk contained numerous treasures, but no-one could get at them, because the Basilisk could kill just by looking at someone. Whoever he looked at turned to stone.

One day, a brave young cobbler decided to capture the treasure guarded over by the Basilisk. After giving a lot of thought to how he would outfox the monster, he took a mirror from one of the Old Town stalls and took it down to the cellar. When he heard the roar of the approaching, he moved the mirror out in front of it. The Basilisk saw its reflection and turned to stone at the sight of its own image. Thanks to his ruse, the clever young cobbler acquired great wealth.

23. Sign depicting the Basilisk off Warsaw's Old Town Marketplace.

24. Golden Duck at Tamka Street fountain.

THE GOLDEN DUCK

Many, many years ago, in the small subterranean lake in the grottos below Ostrogski Palace swam a small duck with golden feathers. It was said to be an enchanted princess who was guarding over immense treasures.

Legends about those treasures abounded amongst the Warsaw townsfolk, but nobody succeeded in capturing them. A poor cobbler decided to search for the treasures, made his way into the grottos and indeed encountered the golden duck The duck proposed a test: the cobbler would get 100 ducats, all of which he must spend before sundown, but only on himself, as he may not share it with others. If he succeeded, he would get the entire treasure. But if he failed, everything he bought would disappear and eh would never again find his way into the grotto. The cobbler agreed to those terms. At sunrise he set out to go shopping. All day he kept spending the money he had got from the duck. He had new, elegant outfits custom-tailored, bought a gold carriage, ate, drank and spent money left and right. Before nightfall he still had one ducat left.

Returning to the palace, he saw an old solider, a war veteran begging for a crust of bread. Seeing him, the cobbler dropped his last coin into the beggar's hat. At that moment, everything he had bought suddenly vanished and he found himself dressed in his old, shabby garb. Since he had not kept his end of the bargain, the magic spell burst. The old solider sympathised with him and consoled him by saying the fortune he earned through honest toil would always be his and would be command the gratitude and respect of others.

THE SECOND WORLD WAR 1939-45

The Second World War 1939-45

On 1st September 1939, German forces launched an assault against Poland, attacking it from three sides. Germany's overwhelming odds soon led to the collapse of Poland's armed resistance. Already on 8th September, Warsaw was attacked by the first German trios if General Reinhardt's Fourth Armoured Division, and by 13th-15th September the entire city was surrounded. Warsaw's mayor and civil-defence commissioner Stefan Starzyński refused to join the evacuation of the Polish government and took command of the city's defence efforts. He became famous for his fiery radio addresses which inspired the nation's spirit of resistance.

Following the Soviet Union's aggression against Poland on 17th September 1939, the Nazis began escalating their war operations. The German-Soviet agreement linked the partition of Poland with the capitulation of its capital. On 17th September, the Germans bombed Warsaw's Royal Castle, and on the 25th carried out carpet bombings which destroyed 12 percent of the city's buildings. 10,000 Warsaw residents perished and 35,000 were wounded as a result.

Warsaw finally capitulated on 28th September, and two days later the first German troops marched into the city. Some 120,000 Polish soldiers were captured. The Nazi occupation, which would be marked by acts of terror, had begun. On 26th October, the Germans created on Polish soil an administrative entity known as the General Government with its capital in

25. Warsaw insurgents emerging from the sewers, 1944.

26. Insurgents "Rybak" and "Kajtek".

Kraków. In reprisal for putting up resistance, Warsaw was to remain in ruins, and the Germans planned to demolish the Royal Castle which had already been damaged by aerial bombings. In accordance with the guidelines Hitler gave General Governor Hans Frank on 4th November, Warsaw was to be reduced to the status of a provincial town. A curfew was imposed, arrests (especially of the Warsaw intelligentsia), executions and deportations to concentration camps got under way. The place political prisoners were detained was Pawiak Prison, from which they were sent to such execution sites in the Warsaw areas as Palmiry. The Gestapo prison at Aleja Szucha was where people caught in street round-ups were tortured.

Nevertheless, the spirit of resistance among the people of Warsaw did not disappear. Already on 27th September 1939 an underground organisation called Polish Victory Service emerged. In November it was renamed the Armed Combat Union under the command of Colonel Stefan Rowecki, cryptonym Grot. By orders of General Władysław Sikorski in 1942, it was transformed into the Home Army.

The Polish Scouting Union, known by the cryptonym Grey Ranks, was also involved in the underground movement. Warsaw may have ceased being the capital of the Polish state, but it became the capital of the Polish Underground State. That clandestine entity issues newspapers, rescued architectural relics, conducted underground educational and cultural activities and, above all, engaged in numerous combat actions and acts of sabotage. Up until 1942, the authorities of the Armed Combat Union promoted passive resistance to the occupation forces to avoid German reprisals against the citizenry. Only limited sabotage and organisational activities were conducted, including the acquisition of weapons, intelligence and counter-intelligence efforts as well as combating informers.

In 1942, the political situation changed. The Germans began suffering defeats on all fronts, and terror against the townspeople of Warsaw was stepped up. As a result, the resistance movement modified its tactics to include more intensive forms of struggle against the occupation forces. In 1943, a structure known as Kedyw was formed within the Home Army to organised armed struggle. The number of armed actions conducted by various units increased and included attacks on Nazi functionaries. One of the most spectacular was the 1944 assassination of General-Major Franz Kutschera, the Warsaw SS and police commander. There were also numerous actions to spring prisoners. The best known occurred outside the arsenal in 1944, when Jan Bytnar was freed from Gestapo detention.

As Soviet forces neared Warsaw, there were fears that Polish territory could become subordinated to the USSR, the more so that on 21st July 1944 a Polish Committee of National Liberation controlled by our eastern neighbour had been set up. The Home Army drew up a plan code-named Storm involving an attack on the Germans' rear lines so as to be able to present themselves to the Soviet authorities as the authentic representatives of the Polish nation. On 26th July, the London-based Polish Government-in-Exile authorised Home Army Commander General Bor-Komorowski to launch an insurrection in Warsaw. When Soviet troops appeared on the outskirts of Warsaw, on 31st July the decision was taken begin the armed struggle the following day at 5 PM, code-named W hour.

In the first days of the struggle, the insurrectionists numbered 50,000. They were armed with only 1,000 rifles, 300 automatic weapons, several grenade launchers, mortars and armour-piercing weapons, 40,000 hand grenades and 12,000 Molotov cocktails. Initially, the German side numbered some 15,000 troops, reinforced on 3rd-4th September by SS and police units. They were superbly armed with heavy and automatic weapons as well as tanks and armoured vehicles. The German forces were concentrated in specially prepared fortified bunkers surrounded by barbed wire. The outbreak of the Warsaw Uprising took Hitler by surprise and infuriated him. In agreement with Himmler, he issued order No. 1 which commanded: "Every inhabitant should be killed. Warsaw is to be levelled to the ground so as to set an intimidating example for all of Europe. And no prisoners of war are to be taken".

At the same time, Stalin, who regarded Warsaw and Fortress Modlin as strategic points, on 5th august had issued an order to halt all military operations on the Warsaw front and intensify efforts in other areas. The Soviets even stopped short of capturing Okęcie Airport, from which air raids against Warsaw had been launched – a move that astonished the Germans themselves. Supply flights by the Western allies were obstructed, and those outlying Home Army units capable of reinforcing the insurgents were particularly combated. Plans to encircle Warsaw were drawn up, but their implementation was

27. Warsaw Uprising. An insurgent in battle.

28. Warsaw Uprising Monument at Krasiński Square.

29. Site commemorating Poles killed during the Nazi occupation.

postponed for five weeks. By the same token, Stalin had sealed Warsaw's fate.

The Germans stationed in Warsaw had obtained information on the outbreak of the uprising. As a result, the initial Polish assault was not as successful as expected. After regrouping, on 5th August the Germans launched a counterattack which forced Polish units to defend isolated districts of the city. They built barricades in the streets and fought over every building and inch of land. The civilian population, including children, took part in the struggle. Unable to quash the rebellion in a single blow, the occupation forces decided on scorched-land tactics. They deployed flame-throwers, artillery and remote-controlled mines of the Goliath and Typhoon type, filled with powerful explosives.

RAF planes, some piloted by Poles, began supply drops to the insurgents on 4th August. Unfortunately, due to heavy plane losses and the limited insurgent-controlled drop areas, of the

30. Warsaw Uprising Museum at Grzybowska Street.

230 tonnes of supplies dropped over Warsaw only less than 50 tonnes reached the Polish freedom-fighters.

On 13th-15th September, the Soviet offensive dislodge the Germans from right-bank Warsaw, and on 16th-22nd September, the 1st Army of the Soviet-backed Polish Armed Forces crossed the Vistula, establishing beach-heads at Czerniaków, Powiśle and Żoliborz. But without the support of the main Soviet forces, the landing proved unsuccessful. The struggle in left-bank Warsaw continued, but the resistance of the insurgents gradually waned, and the Germans succeeded in recapturing one district after another. After the fall of Old Town, the insurrectionists made their way through the sewers to the City Centre, where they continued thee struggle. Żoliborz held out the longest until 30th September.

The act of capitulation was signed on the night of 2nd-3rd October in Ożarów. The insurgent losses were staggering. Of the 50,000 insurrectionists, some 10,000 had been killed, and 25,000 had been wounded. Civilian losses came to 150,000. About 25 percent of the city's buildings had been reduced to rubble, and all its monuments, public buildings and bridges lay in ruins. Following the capitulation, the Germans began demolishing the city with explosives and flame/throwers. By January 1945, 70 percent of the city lay in ruins

The balance-sheet of the Warsaw Uprising is an ambiguous one. It was unique in occupied Europe, since no other city had managed to hold out so long and involve so many residents in the struggle. It was also a desperate attempt to maintain the country's independence against Stalin's imposition of communist rule as symbolised by the Polish Committee of National

31. Home Army Memorial at Jana Matejki Street.

Liberation. But betrayed by its allies in September 1939 and in Teheran in 1943, Poland had no chance of achieving that goal. The spheres of influence had been delimited. All the Polish nation retained was its honour and the message going out into the world: this is how the Polish nation fights for freedom.

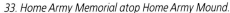

32. Warsaw Heroes' Monument known as the "Warsaw Nike".

33. Home Army Memorial atop Home Army Mound.

THE WARSAW GHETTO

From the first days of the German occupation in Warsaw, people of Jewish ancestry were subjected to different treatment than the rest of the local community. The occupiers regarded as Jews all those who had at least three grandparents belonging to a Jewish religious congregation. As a result, many assimilated individuals who regarded themselves as Poles or even espoused the Christian faith suffered persecution. From 1st December 1939, Jews were obliged to wear arm-bands displaying the Star of David which facilitated German harassment and reprisals such as being robbed, beaten are having beards shorn off. Their bank accounts were blocked, Jewish book shops and schools were closed, Jews were banned from travelling by train and a were restricted to special section in Warsaw's trams. Forced labour was imposed for which the only payment was a modest meal. In 1940, anti-Jewish actions financed by the Germans and used for propaganda purposes began. Nevertheless, many people of Jewish ancestry migrated to Warsaw from front areas incorporated into the Reich and from outlying areas. Round the start of 1940, preparations to create a separate district for Jews got under way. A directive of 2nd October 1940, signed by Governor Fischer, ordered all Jews to be moved into the ghetto. On 16th November, the Jewish Residential District was surrounded by a three-metre-tall wall topped with barbed wire. About 450,000 Jews were herded into an area of some 307 hectares. It consisted of two parts: the big ghetto and the little ghetto, linked by a wooden foot bridge over Chłodna street which was part of the Arian district. Administrative

20

34. Arm-band vendor in the ghetto, 1940.

35. Ruins of the Warsaw Ghetto.

36. Ruins of the Warsaw Ghetto.

37. Warsaw Ghetto. The bodies of murdered Jews, April 1943.

duties were entrusted to the Jewish Council or Judenrat and the Jewish Order-Keeping Service, a hated police formation which took orders from the German authorities. The living and sanitary conditions in the ghetto were deplorable. With 146,000 inhabitants per square kilometre, things were congested and there were eight to ten people per room. Refuse was not removed, causing the spread of various diseases. Often corpses were not buried for several days. The property of ghetto inhabitants had been confiscated and they had no source of income. Food rations were often less than 200 calories a day, so people's main preoccupation was finding something to eat. There was large-scale smuggling by criminal gangs. Help came from beyond the ghetto, smuggled in through tunnels, openings in the wall or by bribed German policemen. Especially useful in such proceedings were Jewish children who could easily come and go through openings and

38. Jews being led out of the ghetto.

39. Wall of the Warsaw Ghetto, 1945.

sewers. Children were also smuggled out of the ghetto, and in that wave their lives were saved. Mortality in the ghetto was extremely high, and by July 1942 some 100,000 people had died. On 22nd July 1944, a cordon of German and Jewish police surrounded the ghetto and announced the compulsory removal of its population "to the east". Everyone was allowed to take along 15 kilograms of luggage, money and valuables.

A daily quota was initially set at 6,000 people and subsequently increased. The operation was conducted in such a way that one by one buildings or sections of the ghetto were surrounded and all its tenants were thrown out of their flats. Anyone who resisted was killed on the spot. Columns of people were formed and driven to what was known as the Umschlagplatz (reloading point) at Stawki Street, connected by a side track to Gdańsk Railway Station. People were beaten with batons, shoved and herded into cattle wagons headed

40. Surviving fragment of the Warsaw Ghetto at Sienna Street.

42. Warsaw Ghetto Memorial in 1945.

41. Nożyk Synagogue.

43. Warsaw Ghetto Heroes Monument.

44. Memorial bunker from which Mordechaj Anielewicz commanded the uprising.

east. The few that managed to flee from the transport after several days brought the tragic news that the trains were travelling to Treblinka Station not far from the town of Małkinia, where a mass-extermination camp fitted with gas chamber had been set up. The trains retuned to Warsaw empty. In spite of that information, the Jewish population passively went to its death. After the Germans announced that everyone who volunteered would get three kilos of bread and jam for the road and that families would not be separated, crowds of starving, sick people came forward. The first to be transported were those of no use to the German war machine. Entire shelters, hospitals and children's care institutions were

evacuated. It was on 5th August 1942 that Janusz Korczak, the outstanding writer and pedagogue, went to his death at the head of columns of children from his orphanage. In September, Judenrat employees and members of the Jewish police were carted away despite the fact that they had served the Nazis.

The deportation campaign lasted until 21st September 1942 and involved some 310,000 Jews. Following that action, only some 30,000 people holding able-bodied worker's certificates and as many more living there illegally remained in the ghetto. On 16th April, Himmler ordered the liquidation of the entire ghetto. On 18th April, the Germans tried to carry out another evacuation but met with active resistance which by the following day had escalated into an open revolt. The resistance put up by Jewish units took the Germans completely by surprise. By 2 PM all the German troops were driven out of the ghetto, suffering serious losses. The Germans changed their tactics and decided to demolish and torch the buildings in the ghetto one by one. The glow of fires could be seen over the city. The new method was producing results. On 8th May, the bunker housing the Jewish Combat Organisation's headquarters, commanded by Mordechaj Anielewicz, was discovered. Unable to mount a defence, he committed suicide. On 16th May, German commander Colonel Jürgen Stroop ordered the Great Synagogue at Tłomackie Street to be blown up, proclaiming that the day the Warsaw Residential District was destroyed. The Warsaw Ghetto was levelled to the ground with the exception of several churches and Pawiak Prison. Most of the ghetto's inhabitants had been killed in the fighting or were taken to Majdanek where they were put to death in gas chambers. Only a small group of fugitives, who had made it over to the Polish side, managed to survive.

45. Umschlagplatz monument.

WARSAW MERMAID

46. Initial location of the Mermaid in the Old Town Marketplace.

47. Mermaid statue on Karowa Street viaduct.

The emblem of the City of Warsaw depicts a being that is half-woman and half-fish, holding a sword aloft in her right hand and a shield in her left. Initially, the emblem had had quite a different appearance. Presumably, it had followed the mediaeval fashion of selecting mythical creatures to symbolise newly emerging towns. The symbol of Warsaw was believed to have been taken from the 2nd-century compilation 'Physiologus' and depicted a creature with the claws of a bird and a scaly dragon's torso. Such was the image of the first known emblem of Old Warsaw dating from 1390. Feminine features emerged in a seal from 1459, however

48. The Syrena (Mermaid), a motorcar produced by Warsaw's FSO factory from 1957 to 1983.

49. Mermaid-shaped fountain, designed by Ryszard Kozłowski, at the Za Żelazną Bramą (Iron Gate) housing estate.

the image of a woman with a fish tail, sword and shield did not appear until 1622. The official emblem in force today, resulting from a 1938 competition, was restored after 1990, when the crown removed during the communist era was replaced.

Warsaw's Mermaid Monument was created in 1855 at the sculpting studio of Konstanty Hegel. It had stood in the Old Town Marketplace until 1928 and was subsequently relocated on several occasions until the year 2000, when it returned to the marketplace.

The Mermaid Monument in Powiśle was created in 1939 at the initiative of Warsaw Mayor Stefan Starzyński. It became associated with the no longer existing Mermaid Bridge (Most Syreny) which was replaced by the Swietokrzyski Bridge. That statue was the work of Ludwika Nitschowa, and 23-year-old Warsaw University student Krystyna Krahelska served as her model. Serving as a field nurse, she was killed in the first days of the 1944 Warsaw Uprising.

50. Mermaid on the PKO building at Czackiego Street.

51. Mermaid at the Wybrzeże Kościuszkowskie riverside.

THE PALACE OF CULTURE AND SCIENCE

The Palace of Culture and Science

52. *Palace of Culture and Science.*

53. *The niches and columns of the Palace of Culture and Science are adorned with 28 allegorical statues symbolising Learning, Art, Sport and Collective Economy.*

   The tallest building in Warsaw is the Palace of Culture and Science. And, regardless of what most Warsovians thought of it, it has became a symbol of Warsaw. It was built in 1952-1955 for Polish money but according to Soviet blueprints and with the aid of Soviet workers. It was to have been a gift of the Soviet Union to Warsaw, and initially it bore the name of Joseph Stalin. But for

54. *The Palace of Culture and Science under construction.*

55. Congress Hall.

many Poles it became the symbol of the Soviet domination of Poland. A typical example of socialist realist architecture with an admixture of art déco and Polish historicism, the building was patterned on the skyscrapers of Chicago and Moscow.

It was designed by Soviet architect Lev Rudnev. At present, the Palace of Culture houses the head offices of various firms as well as such public institutions as cinemas, theatres, art galleries and academic schools. A look-out terrace on the building's 30th floor affords the most beautiful view of Warsaw, because - as Warsovians put it - one can't see the Palace of Culture from there.

56. Attic of the Palace of culture patterned on the attics of Kraków's Drapers' Hall.

57. Warsaw panorama as seen from the look-out terrace of the Palace of Culture.

OLD TOWN

1. King Sigismund III column
2. Royal Castle
3. Mermaid
4. Cathedral
5. Church of Our Lady of Grace

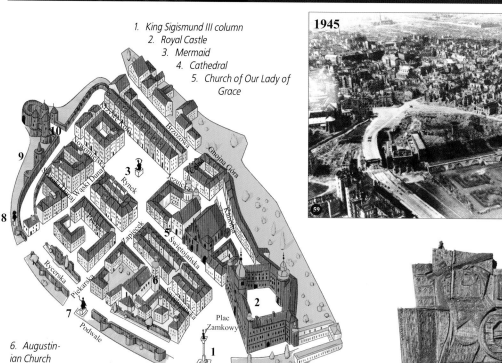

1945

6. Augustin-
   ian Church
7. Kiliński monument
8. Monument to a Young
   Freedom-Fighter
9. Gunpowder Bastion
10. Barbican

58-59. Old Town marked the start of Warsaw's urban development. The town's incorporation and the bringing-in of settlers round the turn of the 14th century was the work of Duke Bolesław II of Płock. Forty parcels of land were mapped out in a chessboard pattern round the square marketplace. By the end of the 14th century, the town was enclosed by a defensive wall independent of the castle's fortifications. At that time, the entire town occupied an area of 10 hectares and counted several hundred inhabitants. Over the centuries there appeared numerous structures that were to give Old Town its unique flavour. The inclusion of Warsaw's Old Town on UNESCO's World Heritage List attests to that fact.

29

60, 63. The Old Town Marketplace is the place most frequented by Warsaw inhabitants and visitors alike. It was created when the town became incorporated towards the end of the 13th century. Round its rim the town's wealthiest patricians built their homes. The most interesting ones were built in the 18th century. The marketplace once contained a town hall, town scales and merchants' stalls.

61. The Statue of the Mermaid, the symbol of Warsaw, was unveiled in the Old Town Marketplace in 1855. Konstanty Hegel drew his inspiration from earlier portrayals of the half-woman/half-fish dating from the 14th century.

62. Two cast-iron wells in the marketplace date from the late 18th century.

1945

64-65. Built in the early 16th century by vintner Grzegorz Korb, Fukier House at No. 27 had housed a popular wine vault from 1590. In 1810, the house was purchased by the Fukier Family. Today one of Warsaw's best restaurants is located there.

66. The origins of St Ann House date from the 15th century, as attested to by such preserved elements as the remnants of Gothic walls and Gothic portals. Its name comes from the 16th century statue of St Ann, the mother of the Blessed Virgin, enshrined in a corner niche.

67. Simonetti House greets people entering the marketplace with its historic clock.

68. The Little Negro Boy House was built at the start of the 17th century for Italian merchant Jakub Gianotti. The head of the Negro boy was meant to symbolise the business of the house owner who dealt in overseas goods.

69. Lion House (No. 13 Old Town Marketplace) dates from the 15th century. It owes its name for the bas-relief of a lion affixed to the first floor in the 18th century. Artist Zofia Stryjeńska's 1928 polychromy, representing the Polish version of art déco, has survived.

70. Ship House at No. 31 Świętojańska Street was built in 1642. Re-modelled in the first half of the 18th century by merchant Łukasz Łyszkiewicz, it was enhanced with a Renaissance portal sporting the bas-relief of a ship, a symbol of trade.

71. The double portal of Wilczkowski House (No. 21 Marketplace) dates from 1608, when Warsaw Old Town Mayor Paweł Zembrzuski built his seat there. The 18th-century political reformer Hugo Kołłątaj had lived and died in the house.

72. Salwator (Saviour) House, built in 1632, owes its name to the figure of Christ set on its attic's axis. The portal's keystone contains the initials of its first owner, Jakub Gianotti.

1939

1945

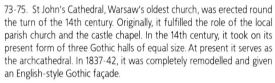

73-75. St John's Cathedral, Warsaw's oldest church, was erected round the turn of the 14th century. Originally, it fulfilled the role of the local parish church and the castle chapel. In the 14th century, it took on its present form of three Gothic halls of equal size. At present it serves as the archcathedral. In 1837-42, it was completely remodelled and given an English-style Gothic façade.

76. Tombstone of the last Dukes of Masovia, Stanislaus and Janusz, the sons of Conrad of Masovia, at St John's Cathedral. It is Masovia's oldest surviving example of a Renaissance-style tomb sculpture. Made of "royal" red Hungarian marble, it was executed in 1526 by the Italian Beranrdinus Zanobi de Gianotis.

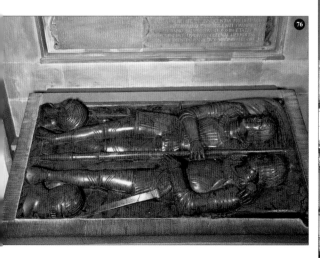

1945

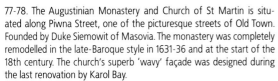

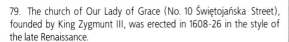

77-78. The Augustinian Monastery and Church of St Martin is situated along Piwna Street, one of the picturesque streets of Old Town. Founded by Duke Siemowit of Masovia. The monastery was completely remodelled in the late-Baroque style in 1631-36 and at the start of the 18th century. The church's superb 'wavy' façade was designed during the last renovation by Karol Bay.

79. The church of Our Lady of Grace (No. 10 Świętojańska Street), founded by King Zygmunt III, was erected in 1608-26 in the style of the late Renaissance.

80. The arcaded passageways that once led from the Castle to the parish church were created for the safety of King Zygmunt following an attempt on his life.

81. Kanonia is a small triangular square on the site of a former graveyard. It owes its name to the dwelling-houses along its rim which were once inhabited by canons of the Warsaw chapter.

82. Dawna Street, linking Jezuicka and Brzozowa Streets, is an example of the atmospheric alleyways of Old Town.

83. Dung Hill is a look-out point at th4e end of Brzozowa Street. The name came from a mediaeval refuse heap found at that spot. One got to it through Dung Gate, whose remnants are found in the house at the corner of Celna and Brzozowa Streets.

84. Brzozowa Street originally lay beyond the town walls, presumably on the site of a refuse dump. Later it led to the Bridge Bastion.

85. Stone Steps are one of the most picturesque Old Town pasage-ways. Originally, water from the Vistula was carried up the steps through a no longer existing White Gate.

86. Szeroki Dunaj Street is a small square that took its name from a stream called Dunaj originating there. Originally a fish market was situated there, and later a flower market. Butchers' Gate, which leads through the walls to Podwale Street, got its name from the area's once numerous butchers' stalls.

87-88. Gunpowder Bastion is a part of the town's preserved defensive walls. Built from the mid-14th to the mid-16th century, they comprised a double ring of fortified walls, bolstered at intervals by bastions and towers.

89. A wall clock featuring a glass mosaic adorns the 18th-century building that now houses the Museum of Artistic and Precision Crafts.

90. The Barbican, which provided additional fortification to the New Town Gate, was built in 1548 by Jan Baptysta of Venice. It was the youngest element of the town's fortifications and originally included a drawbridge. At present, it is a summer arts and crafts gallery.

ROYAL CASTLE

91-93. The Royal Castle was built for King Zygmunt III Vasa after Poland's capital had been moved to Warsaw. The construction of a new residence on a pentagonal plan was entrusted to Italian architects, Giovanni Trevano, Giacomo Rodondo and Matteo Castelli. The castle underwent numerous renovations and expansion schemes in the centuries that followed. Burnt in 1939, its flame-gutted ruins were blown up in 1944. The castle was rebuilt through public donations in 1971-84.

1939

1945

94. Towering above the castle entrance is Zygmunt's Tower, also known as Clock Tower after the clock installed there in 1622. Its mechanism was the work of watchmaker Gerardo Priami who was specially brought in from Florence.

95. Władysław Tower, set on a circular foundation, was built onto the Great House in 1569-71. Renovated in the Baroque style during the reign of King Władysław IV, it was given a portal (1637-43), designed by Battista Gisleni.

96. The Royal Castle's Vistula-side façade was designed by Gaetano Chiveri and built in 1741-46 by Anotnio Solari during the reign of King August III. With its front now turned towards the Vistula, the Castle was endowed with a rococo façade decorated with the sculptures of Jan Jerzy Plersch.

97. The Grodzka Tower from mid 14th century is the oldest part of the Royal Castle.

98. The Castle Gardens once stretched between the Royal Castle and the Vistula, covering an area of 5.8 hectares. The reconstruction project conducted from 1991 has created a different style at each of its three levels. At the highest level are the Baroque-style Vasa Gardens; at the middle level, above Kubicki's Arcades, is a 19-th-century hanging garden; and at the bottom level - a geometric lay-out from the pre-World War Two period.

99. The ballroom was created in a wing built on during the reign of King August III. It was fitted and appointed in 1777-81 at the behest of King Stanisław August Poniatowski according to a design by Dominik Merlini, the chief royal architect. In addition to its superb sculpted decorations, the ballroom is crowned by a 150 square metre plafond painted by Marcello Bacciarelli.

100. Knights' Hall was created during the castle's renovation carried out by royal architect Dominik Merlini in 1774-77. Statues of Chronos and Glory are found in the hall, situated next to the Throne Room.

101. Saxon-style breaks were introduced to the Throne Room during the renovation commissioned by King Stanisław August Poniatowski in 1774-77.

102. During the renovation carried out in the times of King Stanisław August Poniatowski, a conference room containing the portraits of the then crowned heads of Europe was created next to the Throne Room.

103. The castle's Royal Chapel was built during renovations directed by Dominik Merlini in 1774-77.

104. The interior décor of the Royal Castle's Marble Room was created during the reign of King Wadysław IV, the son of King Zygmunt III. During the castle's major renovation undertaken by King Stanisław August Poniatowski, a portrait gallery of Polish kings, painted by Marcello Bacciarelli, was added.

105. The Royal Castle's Canaletto Hall was also created during the Stanislavian period. Appointed and decorated by Dominik Merlini, it features 23 Warsaw landscapes by Italian painter Bernardo Bellotto, known as Canaletto.

106. The ducal cellars are part of the Great Manor erected at the start of the 15th century during the time of Duke Janusz I the Elder. In addition to the duke's chambers, the structure housed the halls in which the ducal council, law courts and the duchy's general assemblies deliberated. The ducal cellars display a cross-vaulted ceiling supported by an octagonal pillar.

107. After 1722, during the reign of King August II, the Senate Hall was moved from the ground floor of the Great Court to the first floor, where its windows opened on today's Castle Square. The hall's décor was designed by Saxon architect Joachim Daniel Jauch.

New Town

108

1. Pauline Church of the Holy Ghost
2. Dominican Church of St Hyacinth
3. St Casimir's Church
4. New Town Square

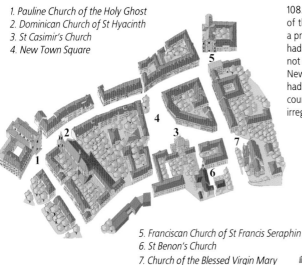

108. New Town developed beyond the New Town Gate round the turn of the 15th century along the road to Zakroczym. On the strength of a privilege granted in 1408, it became an independent urban entity. It had its own marketplace, town hall of municipal authorities, but was not surrounded by fortifications. It was joined to Warsaw in 1791. The New Town Marketplace had originally been rectangular in shape and had covered nearly twice the area of the Old Town Marketplace. In the course of successive modernisations the marketplace took on an irregular shape.

5. Franciscan Church of St Francis Seraphin
6. St Benon's Church
7. Church of the Blessed Virgin Mary

109-110. St Casimir's Church of the Sisters of the Blessed Sacrament was founded by Queen Marysieńka Sobieska. Built in 1688-89, it was an outstanding achievement of architect Tylman of Gameren.

111. Following the destruction caused by the Second World War, only houses of worship were rebuilt in their original form. The townhouses surrounding the marketplace merely reflected the spirit of the many-storied ones built at the start of the 19th century. Stylised polychromy and sgraffita adorn their façades.

112. The Church of the Blessed Virgin Mary is Warsaw's oldest preserved church. Its construction got under way in 1411 at the behest of the Anna Danuta Kiejstut, wife of Masovia's Duke Janusz the Elder and wa completed in 1492.

113. St Benon's Church, built in the 17th century, was given to the Redemptorist Order in 1787 by King Stanisław August Poniatowski. The order set up orphanages which were later converted into craft workshops.

41

114-115. The Franciscan Church of St Francis Seraphic was built in 1680--1733 according to a design by Jan Chrzciciel Ceroni. In 1788, Józef Boretti remodelled its façade and elevated its tower.

116. The Rococo Sapieha Palace (No. 6 Zakroczymska Street) was built in 1731-46 by architect Jan Zygmunt Deybel for the chancellor of the Grand Duchy of Lithuania, Jan Fryderyk Sapieha. Re-modelled in the 19th century, it served as military barracks.

117-118. The building in which Maria Skłodowska-Curie was born in 1867 and live until she was 24 at No. 16 Freta Street now houses a museum in her honour. It contains mementoes linked to the Nobel Prize laureate, including photographs, documents and medals.

119. Freta Street, New Town's high street, leads from the Barbican along the marketplace to the boundaries of that part of town. Originally, this was the road to Zakroczym, round which the town developed. Situated there are the Pauline, Dominican and Franciscan churches, and wealthy burghers built impressive town houses and palaces in the quarter.

120-122. The Dominican Church of St Hyacinth was built in 1612-38 according to the partially Gothic-influenced design of Italian architect Jan Włoch.

1945

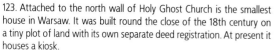

123. Attached to the north wall of Holy Ghost Church is the smallest house in Warsaw. It was built round the close of the 18th century on a tiny plot of land with its own separate deed registration. At present it houses a kiosk.

124. Like the Old Town Marketplace, New Town, in particular Freta Street, attracts tourists with its numerous cafés, restaurants and pubs. Umbrella-shaded cafés appear in the summer months.

125-127. The Pauline Church of the Holy Ghost was built in 1699-1717 according to a design by Józef Piolo and Józef Szymon Bellotti. King Jan Kazimierz granted the site to the Pauline Fathers after the Swedish "deluge" (invasion).

44

128. Steeply descending Mostowa Street once led to a bridge on the Vistula and farther on to the right-bank Praga district. By the 18th century is had been built up with dwelling-houses.

129-130. Raczyński Palace (No. 7 Długa Street) was the work of the superb royal architect, Jan Chrystian Kamsetzer, in 1786. At present, the building houses the Old State Archives, where the oldest and most valuable state documents have been stored for 170 years. They include the original of the Third of May Constitution. On the first floor of the palace is an early-classicist ballroom.

131. A dwelling-house (Mostowa Street) displaying classicist features built in the 18th century. Destroyed in the Second World War, it was rebuilt in 1957.

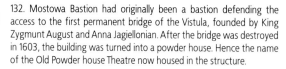

1945

132. Mostowa Bastion had originally been a bastion defending the access to the first permanent bridge of the Vistula, founded by King Zygmunt August and Anna Jagiellonian. After the bridge was destroyed in 1603, the building was turned into a powder house. Hence the name of the Old Powder house Theatre now housed in the structure.

133-134. The Church of Our Lady Queen of the Polish Crown (Krasiński Square) was built in 1660-82 by Tytus Buratini and in 1758-69 was given a new Palladian façade by Jakub Fontana. At present the church is the Field Cathedral of the Polish Armed Forces and the seat of their Chaplain General.

135-136. The Church of St John the Divine (No. 12 Bonifraterska Street) was built in 1726 roku according to a design by Józef Fontana and Antoni Solari. Next to it, one of Poland's first mental hospitals was built.

137. In the 17th century, a small structure (Zakroczymska Street) was built over a spring known for its fine-tasting water. In 1771, it was rebuilt at the behest of King Stanisław August Poniatowski.

138-139. The fortress known as the Citadel (No. 1 Skazańców Street) was erected by Russia's Tsar Nicholas I in 1832-36 directly after the falls of the anti-Russian November Insurrection. Its purpose was to discourage Warsovians from any future upheavals. At present, it houses a section of the Independence Museum. Its most interesting exhibit is a horse-draw prison van in which exiles were sent to Siberia.

140. The Execution Gate on the eastern side of the Warsaw Citadel is a cemetery-mausoleum of political prisoners from the times of the Congress Kingdom. In 1866, a gallows was set up on the terrace, whose remanants may be seen embedded in the gate's walls. The bodies of the executed were secretly buried on the Citadel's slopes.

ROYAL WAY

Royal Way

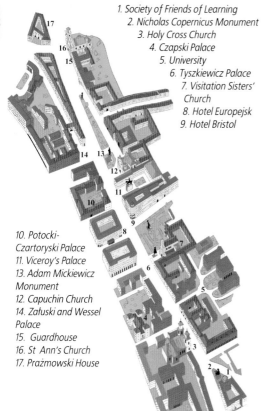

1. Society of Friends of Learning
2. Nicholas Copernicus Monument
3. Holy Cross Church
4. Czapski Palace
5. University
6. Tyszkiewicz Palace
7. Visitation Sisters' Church
8. Hotel Europejsk
9. Hotel Bristol

10. Potocki-Czartoryski Palace
11. Viceroy's Palace
13. Adam Mickiewicz Monument
12. Capuchin Church
14. Załuski and Wessel Palace
15. Guardhouse
16. St Ann's Church
17. Prażmowski House

1945

141-143. The Royal Way was a route created in the 17th century that led from the Royal Castle (Krakowskie Przedmieście Street, photo 143) to the summer palace of King Stanisław August Poniatowski in Łazienki Park. It was along that route, leading via Czersk to Kraków, that Old Warsaw first developed.

144. The Sheet-Metal-Roofed Palace was built in 1720 for Jerzy Dominik Lubomirski and his wife, Magdalena of Tarło. During the times of Prince Józef Poniatowski, its interior appointments were designed by Dominik Merlini. The name of the palace came from what at that time was a rare roofing material.

145. The figure of a female vendor, sculpted by Barbara Zbrożyna, graces Mariensztat Square.

146. Mariensztat, situated behind St Ann's Church at the foot of the escarpment, developed on the site of a jurisdiction (private town) belonging to Maria Potocka. An open-air market existed there from 1847 to 1944. After the war, it was rebuilt in a totally new form, when what was then the modern East-West Thoroughfare was being constructed.

147. The East-West Thoroughfare, the post-war Warsaw's first major town-planning project, was built in 1947-49.

148. The Water Chamber Building, designed and built in 1832 by Alfons Kropiwnicki, has its counterpart on the opposite side of the Vistula.

149. Maria Skłodowska-Curie began her research in the building of a former guardhouse, built in 1818-21 by Chrystian Piotr Aigner.

150. Prażmowski House, built in the latter half of the 17th cetury for royal physician Pastorius, owes its rococo appearance to Jakub Fontana.

151. St Ann's Church, founded in 1454, was a Gothic edifice. A new Baroque-style church designed by Józef Szymon Belotti was built round it in 1660-67. Its classicist façade was designed by Piotr Aigner.

152. The Baroque interior of St Ann's Church features illusion-producing frescoes, painted by Bernardine monk Walenty Żebrowski, as well as rococo altars. Worthy of note are the chapels to Blessed Ładysław of Gielniów and Our Lady of Loretto.

153. The name deanery given to this classicist dwelling-house came from the position held by its first owner, the dean of the collegiate chapter of St John.

154. The statue of Our Lady of Passau was erected by Szymon Bellotti in 1683 as a votive offering for being saved from the plague and in the intention of King John III Sobieski's victory in Vienna. In 1880, two stylised lanterns designed by Józef Dietrich, were added.

155. Rokokowy Załuski and Wessel Palace, erected in the first half of the 18th century, had originally housed a post office.

156-157. Kozia Street emerged in the 14th century when the Czersk Road (Krakowskie Przedmieście) was joined to Senatorska Street.

1945

158-159. The Capuchin Church of the Assumption of the Blessed Virgin Mary and St Joseph was built in 1661-82. Its 1782 façade, the work of Efraim Schroeger, was one of the

160. The Viceroy's Palace, also known as Radziwiłł Palace, owes its reconstruction of 1818-19 to Chrystian Piotr Aigner. Today it is the residence of Poland's president. In front of the palace stands a monument to Prince Józef Poniatowski sculpted by Bertel Thorvaldsen.

161-162. Potocki-Czartoryski Palace in its present late-Baroque form emerged in the 1660 s. Szymon Bogumił Zug and Jan Chrystian Kamsetzer designed its interior for Princess Izabela Lubomirska. Two decorative grates, executed according to the 1896 drawings of Leonard Marconi, grace the palace entrance.

163. In 1765-66 a guardhouse designed by Szymon Bogumił Zug was built in front of the Potocki palace.

164-165. The neo-Renaissance building of the Hotel Bristol was built in 1899-1901 according to a design by Władysław Marconi. The secessionist interior decorations were designed by Viennese architect Otto Wagner the Younger.

166-167. The Hotel Europejski, erected in 1855-77 according to the neo-Renaissance design of Henryk Marconi, was Warsaw's first modern hotel.

168. The Edgeless House, a building of the Military Lodgings Fund, was built in 1933-35 according to blueprints drawn up by Czesław Przybylski. It got its name from the words of Marshal Piłsudski, who reportedly told the building workers: "You gents had better build it without any edges" - a play on the Polish word "kant" which can mean both an edge and a scam.

169-170. The Visitation Sisters' Baroque-style Church of the St Joseph was the creation of Karol Bay in 1728-33. Its unusual façade and interior were designed somewhat later by Efraim Schroeger. The main altar came from the workshop of Jan Jerzy Plersz. Many valuable paintings have been preserved in the church including Tadeusz Kuntze-Konicz's Visitaiton in the main altar and Daniel Szulc's St Louis Gonzaga.

171. Czapski Palace was built according to a design by Tyman of Gameren c. 1690. The building was given the late-Baroque form of a one-storey palace with four alcoves, thanks to the renovation carried out in 1714-22 by Karol Bay and Augustyn Locci. Three decades later, Jan Chrystian Kamsetzer remodelled it in a classicist vein.

172-173. Tyszkiewicz Palace was built by Jan Chrystian Kamsetzer for Ludwik Tyszkiewicz in 1785-92. It later became the property of the Potockis. At present, it houses the special collections of Warsaw University: drawings and old prints. From the street side, Tyszkiewicz Palace is adorned by a stone balcony supported by four figures of Atlas, created in 1787. Their creator was the outstanding royal sculptor, Andrzej Lebrun.

174, 176. The neo-Renaissance building of the Warsaw University Library was erected in 1891-99.

175. The neo-Baroque main gate of the University was erected in 1900.

177. Warsaw University was Warsaw's first institution of higher learning. It was established in 1816 at the initiative of such people as Stanisław Staszic. Kazimierz Palace, now the seat of the university's rector and senate, was built for King Władysław IV and later renovated for King Jan Kazimierz.

178-179. The present Holy Cross Church was built in 1682-96 according to a design by Józef Szymon Belotti. In 1726-54, the Brothers Fontana erected a façade adorned with the figures of the Apostles Peter and Paul, the work of sculptor Jan Jerzy Plersz. Inside, affixed to a pillar is a plaque commemorating Fryderyk Chopin and beneath it - an urn containing his heart. The statue of Christ carrying His cross was sculpted by Andrzej Pruszyński in 1858.

180. The Polski Theatre building (No. 2 Karasia Street) was erected in 1912 roku according to a design by Czesław Przybylski at the imitative of Arnold Szyfman who went on to become its long-standing director. Its inauguration was marked by a performance of Zygmunt Krasiński's "Irydion" in 1913.

181-182. The classicist edifice of the Society of Friends of Learning was built in 1820-23 according to Antonio Corazzi's design and is known as Staszic Palace after the name of its founder. In 1892-93, the palace was renovated in the Byzantine-Ruthenian style, reflecting the Russification policy of the Russian occupation forces (illustration 181).

183. Ostrogski Palace is the seat of the Fryderyk Chopin Society which gathers mementoes and documents relating to Poland's world-renowned composer. The late-16th-century palace, which underwent numerous renovations including that carried out by Józef Fontana in 1752, acquired its present appearance in the 19th century.

184. Baroque-style Zamoyski Palace, built in 1878-1879 by Leonardo Marconi, was endowed with the then fashionable "French costume" - the Renaissance style typical of the reigns of Henry IV and Louis XIII.

185. Next to Zamoyski Palace stands Przeździecki Palace, built in 1878-1879 by architect Marceli Berent.

186. Kossakowski Palace at No. 19 Nowy Świat Street took on its present form in 1848. Its then owner, Władysław Pusłowski, had Henryk Marconi renovate the existing palace in the neo-Renaissance style. Franciszek Maria Lanci was responsible for its interior décor. Warsaw's first artificial ice-rink was opened in the palace gardens in 1912.

187-188. Nowy Świat Street is an important stretch of the Royal Way. Not built up until the end of the 18th century, it boasts many interesting dwelling-houses and palaces.

1945

ALEJE UJAZDOWSKIE

189. In 1731, Stations of the Cross were laid out on the west side of Ujazdów. It led from Three Crosses Square to the wooden church at Ujazdów. In 1770, the station was dismantled to make way for a Baroque-style urban-development project which acquired its present name before 1784. In the 1830s, the elegant mansions of the Warsaw aristocracy began arising there. Soon Aleje Ujazdowskie would become Warsaw' summer salon.

190-191. At the centre of Three Crosses Square stands ther Classicist Church of St Alexander, designed by Chrystian Piotr Aigner and built in 1818-26. The cupolated rotunda alludes to the Pantheon of Rome.

192. The Polish Sejm (parliament) Building was erected in 1925-28 according to the design of Kazimierz Skurewicz. The semi-rotunda housing its main assembly hall dates from that period.

193. Designed by Pius Dziekoński round the close of the 19th century, the neo-Gothic building (Aleje Ujazdowskie 22) sports an interested glazed-brick façade.

194. Two giants holding up a balcony formed part of the modernistic 'At the Giants' dwelling-house designed by Władysław Marconi in 1904--07.

195. In Mokotowska Street stands a dwelling-house erected in 1900 according to a design by Zygmunt Binduchowski. Its elevation is adorned by figures in Polish folk attire. Pictured is a Polish highlander.

196. Poznański Palace was built in the 19th century.

197. The name of the palazzo "Pod Karczochem" ("Under the Arti-choke") is derived from a restaurant it once housed. The building, pur-chased by architect Henryk Marconi in 1869, was reconstructed in the eclectic style.

198. Sobański Palace is the eclectic 1876 work of Leonardo Marconi and alludes to the Renaissance epoch.

199. The neo-Renaissance building of the Astronomical Observatory was designed by Michał Kado, Hilary Szpilowski and Chrystian Piotr Aigner and built in 1820-24.

200. Classicist Śleszyński Palace (Aleje Ujazdowskie 25) was designed by Antonio Corazzi and built in 1826 for Stanisław Śleszyński. Its owner, a Capitan of the army of the Polish Kingdom, became famous for his recreational garden known as Swiss Valley.

1945

201-202. Ujazdów Castle, perched on the Vistula escarpment, was built on orders from King Zygmunt III Vasa in 1624. It was later remodelled by such famous architects as Tylman of Gameren, Dominik Merlini and Stanisław Zawadzki. Burnt and dismantled down to its foundation, it re-emerged anew in 1973 to serve as a Centre of Contemporary Art.

203-204. Belvedere Palace owes its name to the beautiful view (belle vedere) that can be enjoyed from its garden. Its classicist form was created in 1819-22 by Jakub Kubicki for the tsarist viceroy, Prince Constantine. Between the two World Wars and also at the start of the Third Republic is was the seat of Poland's presidents. Józef Piłsudski, Poland's great pre-war leader, also resided there. His monument has been erected next to the palace.

ŁAZIENKI
Łazienki

205

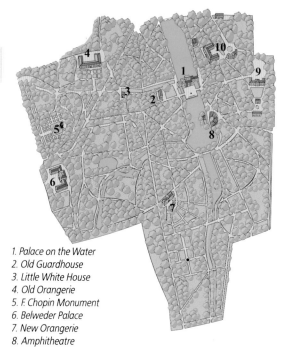

1. Palace on the Water
2. Old Guardhouse
3. Little White House
4. Old Orangerie
5. F. Chopin Monument
6. Belweder Palace
7. New Orangerie
8. Amphitheatre
9. Myślewicki Palace
10. New Guardhouse

206

Łazienki is an original palace and garden complex on a European scale. It was originated by Stanisław Herakliusz Lubomirski who built baths and a hermitage on the grounds of the royal menagerie. Its next owner, King Stanisław August Poniatowski, converted it into his summer residence. From 1766, impressive geometrically landscaped royal gardens were laid out.

205-206. The Palace on the Water is the principal building of Royal Łazienki Park. The original baths, designed by Tylman of Gameren, were built by Stanisław Herakliusz Lubomirski in about 1680. During the reign of King Stanisław August Poniatowski, a classicist palace designed by Dominik Merlini arose. Its northern façade was given a columned portico.

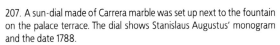

207. A sun-dial made of Carrera marble was set up next to the fountain on the palace terrace. The dial shows Stanislaus Augustus' monogram and the date 1788.

208. In 1793, two pavilions were built and joined to the palace proper by bridges topped with colonnaded galleries. There, peacocks often seek refuge from obtrusive tourists.

209. The classicist Ballroom was added to the palace in 1788. Its décor was the work of Jan Chrystian Kamsetzer.

210. Salomon's Hall is an elegant room reminiscent of a biblical temple. Its walls were adorned with the paintings of Marcello Bacciarelli.

211. The Bath Chamber in the Palace on the Water dates from the Baroque renovation of the Baths under Great Crown Marshall Stanisław Herakliusz Lubomirski. The author of the project was Tylman of Gameren.

63

212

213

212-214. The Little White House, built in 1774-76, was the first structure erected by Stanisław August in the Łazienki grounds. The wooden building, most likely the work of Dominik Merlini, reflects a villa style of architecture. Rich decorative painting adorns its interior. An example is the Dining Room, completely covered with paintings of the grotesque variety created by Jan Bogumił Plersz, which became a model for many later classicist residences.

214

215-216. The Old Orangerie was built according to a design by Dominik Merlini. It houses a theatre, one of the world's few surviving examples of an 18th-century court theatre.

217. The Water Chamber, where water was stored during the times of the Lubomirskis and later piped to the Bath House. It acquired its present shape in 1777-78 thanks to the efforts of Dominik Merlini. It was patterned on the Tomb of Cecilia Meteli in Rome's Appian Way.

218. The classicist Temple of Diana was built in about 1820 to resemble an ancient Greek temple.

219

220

219. The Nowa Kordegarda (new guardhouse) Building, built in 1780, was known as *Trou-Madame*. Today it houses a café by the same name which alludes to its 18th-century tradition.

220. The building of the was built in 1791-92 according to a design by Jan Chrystian Kamsetzer for the royal guard guarding the entrance to the Palace on the Water.

221-222. Myślewicki Palace, whose name comes from the village of Myślewice, was built in 1775-78 according to a design developed by Dominik Merlini. To its sides were added quarter-circular wings ending in pavilions, and thus a palace with classicist features came into being. It survived the Second World War and boasts a splendid interior. Views of Rome and Venice painted by Jan Bogumił Plersz have been preserved in the Dining Room pictured here.

221

222

223-224. The Amphitheatre, inspired by the ancient theatre in Herculanum, was built in 1790-91 according to a design conceived by Jan Chrystian Kamsetzer. The stage on the little island, on which performances take place to this day, was provided with column ruins reminiscent of Jove's Temple in Baalbeck.

225-226. The New Orangerie is situated in the park's southern reaches. It was built in 1860 according to a design developed by Adam Adolf Loeve and Józef Orłowski. In keeping with its original purpose, it houses various exotic plants.

227. In this southern district of Warsaw is found a huge palace-park complex built for King Jan III Sobieski. The original none-too-big manor house called Villa Nova, was transformed into a Baroque-style palatial residence. The oldest part of Wilanów Palace is its main hull. It was built according to a design by Augustyn Locci in 1681-96 for Jan III Sobieski. In 1732-29, wings on both sides of its forecourt were added. Work on the palace continued with interruptions until the end of the 19th century.

228. Wilanów Palace in an 1850 water colour by W. Richter.

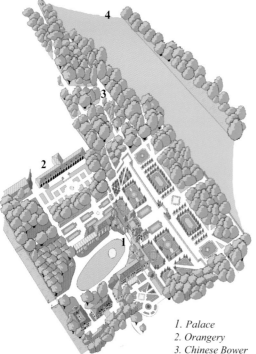

1. Palace
2. Orangery
3. Chinese Bower
4. Roman Bridge

229. The Mausoleum of Stanisław Kostka and Aleksandra Potocki was built in 1836 by their son Aleksander. The neo-Gothic work of Henryk Marconi is adorned with sculptures by Jakub Tatarkiewicz and Konstanty Hegel.

230. St Ann's Church owes its neo-Renaissance appearance to the renovation carried out in 1857-70 under the supervision of Henryk and Leander Marconi and Jan Huss.

231. A bridge over a moat and a monumental 17th-18th-century gate lead to the palace's main entrance.

232. Manège and Coach-house designed by Franciszek Maria Lanci and built in 1848 roku. After the Second World War, only the building's façade survived. A modern pavilion was built onto it, and in 1963 the world's first poster museum was opened there.

233. The garden-side elevation is centrally positioned towards the scenic garden axis running through the park, canal and lanes in Morysin Field.

234. The Queen's bed chamber is one of the palace's most elegant Baroque premises. The ceiling is adorned with an allegorical painting of Spring - the work of Jerzy Eleuter Siemiginowski.

235. A supraporta in the form of a lion's skin symbolises the courage and bravery of King John III Sobieski. It was placed above the doorway of the garden-side wall.

236. The Baroque décor of the King's Bed Chamber is accentuated by a posted bed whose canopy was sewn from Turkish fabric captured by King Jan III Sobieski at the Battle of Vienna.

237. The King's Ante-Chamber is adorned with rich stuccowork and painted decorations. The ceiling is contains a plafond depicting Winter, painted by Jerzy Eleuter Siemiginowski, and the stuccowork was executed by Andrzej Schlüter.

238. In the corridor beneath the south tower of Wilanów Palace is an equestrian monument to John III Sobieski as the conqueror of the Turks. Originally it had stood in the Grand Hall in an alcove opposite the palace entrance. It was made of plaster by an unknown royal artist in 1693.

239. In 1799-1821, Stanisław Kostka Potocki created a romantic scenic park in the northern reaches of Wilanów. The Chinese Bower was put up in 1806.

240. When the palace was being built, a twin level Baroque-style garden was created - the work of Italian Adolfo Boy. The patchwork of lawns and box-shrub-lined lanes was laid out in keeping with the geometric principles of the times.

241. The park's Roman Bridge was built in 1806.

242. In the park's south side is the Orangery, renovated by Chrystian Piotr Aigner. It now houses a Gallery of Contemporary Polish Sculpture.

243-245. Krasiński Palace (Krasiński Square), Warsaw's must splendid secular Baroque edifice, was built in 1677-82 for Jan Dobrogost Krasiński according the a design by Tylman of Gameren The tympanum on the palace side is adorned with the decorative sculptures of Andrzej Schlüter.

1945

246. Mostowski Palace owes its name to Tadeusz Mostowski who in 1823 was responsible in endowing the earlier-built structure with its new classicist form.

247. In front of Muranów Cinema stands a fountain dating from 1866. It was designed by Józef Orłowski and Alfons Grotowski and sculpted by Leonard Marconi. Originally it had been set up in a square at Krakowskie Przedmieście. In 1906-10 it graced Bank Square and has been at its present location since 1947.

248-249. The Church of the Visitation of the Blessed Virgin Mary, erected in 1682-1732, has a main altar founded by Great Crown Hetman Józef Potocki. During a road-widening operation in 1962, the building was moved back 21 metres.

73

250. Bank Square emerged in its present shape in 1951 as Dzierżyński Square. In 1989, the square's former name was restored and some time later a building known as the blue skyscaper was erected, so called because of the azure sky reflected by its mirror-like elevation panels.

251. The Palace of the Commission of Government Revenues and Treasury, now Warsaw's town hall, was built by Antoni Corazzi in 1823-25.

252. The building of the former Polish Bank and Bourse, built by Antonio Corazzi in 1825-28, today is home to the John Paul II Collection of Paintings created by Janina and Zbigniew Porczyński.

253. Two market halls called Hala Mirowska were built in 1899-1901, when the Russian general Nikolai Bibikov was mayor of Warsaw. Based on an earlier concept of Stefan Szyller, they were designed by Bolesław Miłkowski and Ludwik Panczakiewicz.

254. Lubomirski Palace, featuring a portico supported by 10 ionic-columns, was built in its present classicist form in 1791-93 by Jakub Hempel.

255. The Arsenal, currently the Archaeological Museum, was built under the supervision of General Paweł Grodzicki for King Władysław IV.

256. Tepper-Dückert Palace, known as the Four Winds (No. 38/40 Długa Street), was built in the 1680s for Lord High Steward of Bacław, Stanisław Klainpoldt-Małopolskiego. It was thoroughly re-modelled in the classicist style in 1769-80 by Szymon Bogumił Zug.

257. Eagle House was built in 1616-24 for Royal Treasurer Mikołaj Daniłowicz of Żurów. A staircase, portal and frieze with the images of kings have survived from that period. In 1747-94, the building housed the Załuski Public Luirbary, one of the first in Europe.

258. Przebendowski-Radziwiłł Palace, now the Museum of Independence, was built in 1730 according to a design by Jan Zygmunt Deybel.

259. The Basilian Church (No. 16 Miodowa Street), built in 1782-84 after the design of Dominik Merlini, contains paintings created by 18th-century artist Franciszek Smuglewicz.

260. Collegium Nobilium (No. 22/24 Miodowa Street), a school for the sons of aristocrats and wealthy noblemen established in 1740 by Stanisław Konarski, was built in 1743-54. Its 1786 renovation endowed it with classicist features.

261. Bishop Młodziejowski's Palace (Podwale Street) was built towards the end of the 17th century. Remodelled in 1804-11 according to a design by Fryderyk Albert Lessel.

262-263. The Pac-Radziwiłł Palace (No. 15 Miodowa Street) comprises one part built by Tylman of Gameren in 1681-97 for Dominik Mikołaj Radziwiłł and the Ludwik Pac Palace, situated in Miodowa Street, built by Henryk Marconi in 1824-28. The arcaded gate, stylised to resemble a triumphal arch, is adorned with bas-relief-type friezes sculpted by Ludwik Kaufman. The palace boasts splendid interiors: the Mauretanian Hall (pictured) and the Gothic Hall.

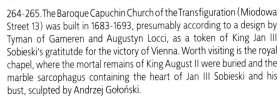

264-265. The Baroque Capuchin Church of the Transfiguration (Miodowa Street 13) was built in 1683-1693, presumably according to a design by Tyman of Gameren and Augustyn Locci, as a token of King Jan III Sobieski's gratitutde for the victory of Vienna. Worth visiting is the royal chapel, where the mortal remains of King August II were buried and the marble sarcophagus containing the heart of Jan III Sobieski and his bust, sculpted by Andrzej Gołoński.

266. A rich Baroque façade graces Loupel Palace (Miodowa Street), built in the mid-18th century. It dates from the building's renovation carried out by S. Zug for Great Crown Chancellor Jacek Małachowski.

267. The rococo-style Branicki Palace, built from 1740 first by Jan Zygmunt Deybel and subsequently by Jakub Fontana, belonged to Jan Klemens Branicki. A lover of art, he imported elements for its interior decoration from Paris.

268. Built in 1593 as the Primate's Palace and entrusted to the Gniezno Chapter, it served as the residence of the Polish primate. The palace owes its present classicist form, including its columned portico and semi-elliptic wings, to the expansion project conceived by Efraim Schroeger.

269-270. Jabłonowski Palace, built in 1768-85 initially by Jakub Fontana and subsequently by Dominik Merlini, was transformed into the Warsaw town hall in 1817-19. The present building of a financial and commercial centre resembles the original structure only through its façade.

271-272. The classicist building of the Wielki Theatre was built in 1825-33 according to a design by Antoni Corazzi, assisted by Ludwik Kozubowski. It boasts Europe's biggest opera stage, can accommodate an audience of 1,900.

1945

273. The Church of the Artistic Community was erected at the site of St Andrew's Church which had been razed in 1953. The façade of the new church, built in 1998-99, only slightly alludes to the original structure's classicist style.

274. Blank Palace was built in 1762-64 in the Baroque style according to a design by Szymon Bogumił Zug for Filip Nereusz Szaniawski. In 1777, the palace was purchased by Piotr Blank, a well-known banker of King Stanisław August's era, who had it remodelled in the classicist mode. At present, it houses the Conservator's Office and the Monument Conservation Workshop.

275-276. Behind an uninteresting façade the Landau Bank, built in 1904-06 for financier Wilhelm Landau, contains a splendid secessionist interior.

277. Mniszech Palace, also known as the Merchants' Club, was built in 1731 by Burchard Krzysztof Münnich for Marshal Józef W. Mniszech. Towards the end of the 18th century, the palace was the seat of a Masonic lodge, hence for a time it was referred to as Lucifer's Palace. In 1820, it became the seat of the Merchants' Club where meetings, lectures and balls were held.

278. The building of the Society for the Encouragement of the Fine Arts (Zachęta) was built according to a design by Stefan Szyller in the academic Renaissance style in 1898-1903. The society was established by Polish painters to popularise contemporary Polish art. The purchase of outstanding art works, moved in 1940 to the National Museum, was organised. Today the building contains an art gallery.

279-280. The classicist Augsburg Evangelical (Lutheran) Church of the Holy Trinity was built in 1777-81 according to a design by Bogumi Zug.

281. The eclectic-style building of the Municipal Credit Society, currently Bank Pekao SA, was built in stages from 1878 to 1911 after a design by Julian Ankiewicz and Władysław Marconi. Its portico's tympanum contains a bas-relief depicting the allegory of Prosperity, the work of Pius Weloński.

282. The building of the Association of Technicians, designed by Jan Fijałkowski, was erected in 1903-05 in the neo-Baroque style.

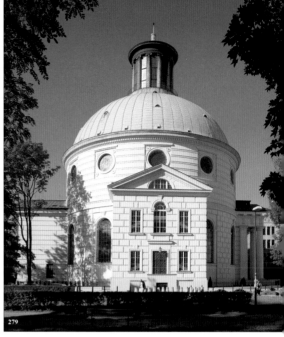

1945

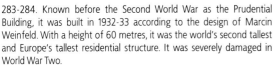

283-284. Known before the Second World War as the Prudential Building, it was built in 1932-33 according to the design of Marcin Weinfeld. With a height of 60 metres, it was the world's second tallest and Europe's tallest residential structure. It was severely damaged in World War Two.

285. The early-Modernist building of the Cooperative Societies Bank known as Eagle House was built in 1913-17 according to the design of Jan Heurich, junior. The eagles with outstretched wings adorning the building as well as bas-reliefs devoted to human toil were the work of Zygmunt Ott.

286. Philharmonic Hall was built in 1900-01 through the patronage of the local aristocracy and bourgeoisie. It was designed by architects Karol Kozłowski and Izydor Pianka.

287. The architecturally eclectic house of the Wedels, a family of sugar and chocolate barons, was built in 1893 and reflected elements of the French Renaissance.

288. The Jabłkowski Brothers Department Store was built in 1913-14 according to a design by Karol Jankowski and Franciszek Lilpop. Its interior features post-secessionist stained-glass windows by Edmund Bartłomiejczak.

289-290. The site of today's Palace of culture and Science before World War Two had been an area of densely built-up tenements lining Zielna, Śliska, Sienna, Chmielna and Złota streets. Traces of those streets may be seen on the commemorative plaques set into the pavement along the paths surrounding the Placa of Culture. Before the war, the area round the entrance to today's suburban-train station had been the site of Warsaw's Central Railway Station, then Europe's most modern train station.

291. The Modernist office building at ulica Wspólna 62 was designed by architect Marek Leykam. The façade reflects the style of the 15th-century Florentine bankers' palace, and its interior was built round a monumental, circular cupola-topped courtyard.

1945

292-293. The Warsaw Metro is one of the world's youngest underground systems. The decision to build it had been taken as far back as 1925, but 15th April 1983 marked the actual start of the building project. At present, the metro transports passengers between Kabaty in the southern suburb of Ursynów to the northern district of Żoliborz.

294-295. Warsaw's longest and best-known street is Marszałkowska, laid out in the mid-18th century at the centre of the Bielino jurisdiction by Marshal Franciszek Bieliński. Known earlier as Bielińska and Otwocka street, it got its present name in honour of Marshal Bieliński in 1770, when it was extended to today's Lublin Union Square (Plac Unii Lubelskiej). In the mid-19th and early 20th centuries, several-storey buildings reflecting historic architectural styles grew up along the thoroughfare. Unfortunately, not many of them managed to survive the Second World War.

1939

296. Built in 1901-11 according to a design of Józef Pius Dziekoński, the Church of the Redeemer reflects architectural elements of the Polish Renaissance and Baroque.

297, 299. Constitution Square was part of the city's socialist realistic development planned during the times of President Bolesław Bierut.

298. The neo-Gothic designed by Pius Dziekoński round the turn of the 20th century gives some idea of how Marszałkowska Street looked back then.

84

1950

300-301. The building of the Warsaw Polytechnic was built in 1899-1901, chiefly by architect Stefan Szyller. Inside is a magnificent four-storey hall fringed with galleries and topped with a skylight.

302. The Water-Filtration Station was built in the 1880 as an element of the first water-main and sewer system in what was then the Russian Empire. It was the creation of Englishman William Lindley and his sons who had built similar facilities in many other European cities.

303. Lwowska Street has retained the architecture of pre-World War Two Warsaw. Shown is the balcony of one of its Art Nouveau tenements.

NEW ARCHITECTURE

304.

305

304. The destruction of World War Two particularly affected the area round today's Palace of Culture and Science. From the 1980s, office towers dominating the city-centre skyline began arising on the site of the war-ravaged pre-war urban tenements.

305. The 153-metre-high Inter Continental is Poland's tallest hotel. It was designed by a team of architects headed by Tadeusz Spychała.

306. In the direct proximity of the Central Railway station is the Złote Tarasy (Golden Terraces) office-shopping-recereational centre. It got its name from Złota Street, where the building was constructed in 2002--07. The generally accessible atrium at its centre is topped by a 10,000 metre^2 undulating roof comprising 4,780 glass triangles with up to 3-metre-long sides.

306

307. The 115-metre-tall Orco Tower was built by an Italian investor in 1992-96.

308. Hotel Marriott (Aleje Jerozolimskie 65/79), which is 170 metres tall, was built in the 1980s. Apart from the hotel, the building's 20 top storeys contain the offices of Polish LOT Airline. Next to it stands the 150-metre-tall Intraco II office tower, built in 1979.

309. Warta Tower Office Building.

310. Warsaw Trade Tower (Chłodna Street 51), which soars to a height of 208 metres, is second only to the Palace of culture as Warsaw's tallest building. Some claim it is the tallest, because if both buildings' spires are ignored, the WTT is actually 3 metres taller than the Palace of Culture. It was built by the South Korea's Daweoo concern in 1997-99.

311. The Polish Telecoms building (No. 14/16 Twarda Street) was built in 2003. Its 30-floor look-out terrace at a height of 128 metres can compete with that of the Palace of Culture.

312. Millennium Plaza (Aleje Jerozolimskie 123), built in 1999 by Turkish investor Vahap Toya, is regarded as one of Warsaw's ugliest buildings.

313. Solniczka Office Tower at Aleje Jerozolimskie.

314. The new State Mint at Żelazna Street 56.

315. Hotel Mercure Fryderyk Chopin (Aleja Jan a Pawła II 22) exemplifies the modern architecture that has made its appearance in Warsaw.

316. The 194-metre-tall Rondo 1 tower was built in 2003-06.

317. The 120-metre-tall high-rise Hotel Westin (Aleja Jana Pawła II 21) was built in 2003. Its rooms are fitted in the style of the 1960s. Its lifts, which attain a speed of 3.5 metres per second, are situated in a glass tube attached to the building's outside wall.

318. Atrium Shopping Mall at the corner of Grzybowska Street and Jana Pawła II Avenue.

319. The Metropolitan office building (at Piłsudski Square) was designed by world-renowned architect Sir Norman Foster and built in 2003.

320. The building of Warsaw University Library (Dobra Street 55/66), completed in 1999, roku, was the work of Marek Budzyński and Zbigniew Badowski. It contains nearly three million volumes.

321-322. The Supreme Court and Appeals Court building was built at Krasiński Square in 1999. It is adorned by "Columns of Law" displaying quotations from Roman law. On the Nowiniarska Street side, three sculptures symbolising Faith, Hope and Charity are reflected by a pool.

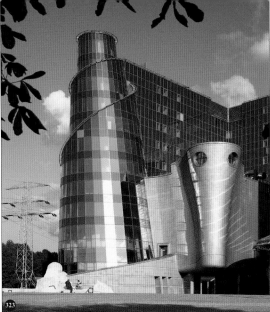

323. Modern Polish Television building at Samochodowa Street in Mokotów district.

324. The Blue Tower was built in 1991 at Bank Square at the former site of the Great Synagogue at Tłomackie Street, destroyed in the last war. Jewish organisations agreed to the skyscraper's construction on condition that it included a hall of Jewish memory.

325. The Olympic Centre (Wybrzeże Gdyńskie 4) was built in Żoliborz district in 2003-04 on a plateau overlooking the Vistula. The modern building was designed by Bogdan Kulczyński and Paweł Pyłek. In front of tis entrance stands a sculpture of Icarus, the work of Igor Mitoraj.

PRAGA

326.

327.

326. Praga, Warsaw's right-bank district, dates from the 10th century, when a fortified defensive settlement was built in Stare Bródno. On the site of a later locality known as Targów, in time a village called Praga was established. It's name came from the practice of burning forests. In the following centuries it broke up into: Episcopal Praga, which received municipal rights in 1648, and Ducal Praga, a privately owned town. The two localities shared a single town hall.

327. Praga market, 1791 painting by Jan Piotr Norblin.

328-329. The Classicist Water Chamber building (Kłopotowskiego Street 1/3), designed by Antonio Corazzi, was built in 1825. It served as a toll-collecting station for travellers using the bridge over the Vistula leading to the foot of Bednarska Street.

328.

329.

330-331. Praga's Cathedral of St Florian, designed in the neo-Gothic style by Józef Pius Dziekoński, was built in 1888-1901. It was elevated to the rank of a cathedral in 1992.

332. The only surviving building of the Praga district's Jewish quarter is the "Mykva" (Kłopotowskiego Street) which once housed ritual baths.

333-335. The Church of Our Lady of Loretto is Praga's oldest house of worship. The Chapel of Loretto, founded by King Władysław, was erected in 1640-44. It was believed to have been designed by Constantino Tencalli on the basis of the chapel in Loretto.

336-337. In Praga, Warsaw's right-bank district, stands the Eastern Orthodox Cathedral of St Mary Magdalene. Built in 1868-69 according to a design by Nikolai Sichev, its architecture displays Byzantine-Ruthenian influence. Worth viewing in its interior is its polychromy and exceptionally decorative iconostasis.

338. The New Shopping Centre was opened in 2002 at the Warszawa Wileńska Railway Station.

339. The Modernist building of the State Railway Authority (Targowa Street 74), designed by Marian Lalewicz, was built in 1928-29. Interesting art déco style décor graces its interior.

340. The tenement building at the corner of Targowa an Ząbkowska streets exemplify the urban structures of old Praga. Genuine 19th-century granite cobbles have survived in Ząbkowska street running past the building.

341-342. The several-storey urban structures of Praga, most of which were not destroyed in the war, give this corner of Warsaw a climate all its own. A typical feature of this neighbourhood are the Praga court-yards with their characteristic religious shrines.

343. One of the most interesting examples of Warsaw's industrial archi-tecture is the Koneser distillery, built in 1867 in what was once the village of Rogatki Ząbkowskie. Some of its buildings now host cultural events.

344. The Basilica of the Most Sacred Heart of Jesus (Kawęczyńska Street 53), funded by Duchess Maria Zawisza-Radziwiłł in 1907-23, al-luded architecturally to Rome's Basilica of St Paul Outside the Walls.

345. The 10th-Anniversary Stadium on the Vistula in Praga's Kamionek quarter was built in 1954-55 as an Olympic stadium accommodating 71,000 spectators. Its rim was built upon the rubble of the city which had been destroyed during the Warsaw Uprising and in the early post-war years. At present, a National Stadium is being built on the site of the 10th-Anniversary Stadium.

346. Grochów Manor (No. 64 Grochowska Street) was built within a park in around 1836 for an industrialist of Swedish ancestry, Karol Osterloff, on the site of a former structure.

347. Różycki's Bazaar - one of Poland's best-known markets - is situated between Targowa and Brzeska streets. It was set up in the mid-19th century on a parcel belonging to financial potentate Julian Różycki, a graduate pharmacist. During the communist period it was one of the few places in Warsaw, where literally 'everything' could be purchased.

348. The Church of the Purest Heart of Mary was built at the site of the Battle of Olszynka Grochowska, fought during the 1830-31 November Insurrection. Construction according to the design of Andrzej Boni was begin in 1934 but not completed until 1941.

389. One of two Grochów toll-houses built in 1823 according to the design of Jakub Kubicki. The structure seen in this photo was moved 10 metres in connection with a road-widening project.

MOKOTÓW

Mokotów

350. The Warsaw district of Mokotów evolved from several villages situated to the south of Old Warsaw. They included Milanowo (Wilanów), Powsino, Mokotowo and Służew. Those names have survived to describe individual sections of Mokotów district. For centuries, those areas had been a favourite location for summer residences, built by the king, aristocrats and better-to-do nobility. The main thoroughfare of Upper Mokotów is Puławska which was part of the road leading via Czersk to Puławy and Lublin.

351. One of Mokotów's toll-gates, whose construction by Jakub Kubicki in 1817 was commissioned by the municipal authorities.

352-354. Szuster's Palace at Puławska Street was designed by Efraim Schroeger and built in 1772-74 for Izabela Lubomirska. Henryk Marconi was responsible for its neo-Gothic renovation in 1821-25. The palace is surrounded by English-style gardens, designed by Szymon Bogumił Zug. Several other structures were built at that time, including the Flemish Glorietta, later known as Flemish House (photo 353), and a tower with pigeon house (photo 352).

355. This Classicist manor house, built around 1840, is a remnant of an that once belonged to Ksawery Pusłowski.

356. The former J. H. Dąbrowski Fort No. 9 in the Sadyba Czerniakowska quarter houses the Katyń Museum of memorabilia left by the POWs murdered by the NKVD in 1940 in Katyń, Kharkov and Mednoe.

357. In 1870, an auberge known as the Yellow Inn was built in the Służew district at Aleja Wilanowska. Designed by Jan Maria Lanci, it alluded to the style of Italian and English suburban villas. At present, the building houses the Historical Museum of the Polish Peasant Movement.

358.

359.

358-359. The Church of St Anthony of Padua in Czerniaków was founded by Stanisław Herakliusz Lubomirski who had owned area estates since 1683. The church, planned as a family mausoleum, was erected 1690-93 by builder Izydor Affaita according to the design of royal architect Tylman of Gameren. Rich Baroque-style stuccowork and frescoes attributed to Antoni Giorgioli or Tylman of Gameren. Before the main altar is a reliquary of St Boniface the Martyr, which Lubomirski had brought from Rome. Adjoining the church is a monastery entrusted to the Bernardine Fathers.

360. The 1818 View of the Church at Czerniaków by Aleksander Majerski.

360.

361. The horse-race track at Służewiec was laid out on a 150-hectare parcel of land, purchased in 1925 by the Society for the Encouragement of Horse Rearing in Poland. The complex was built in 1939 according to the Modernist design of Warsaw architect Zygmunt Plater-Zyberek.

362. A wooden church had stood on the site of St Catherine's Chruch as early as 1238. Its present neo-Romanesque style dates from the renovation carried out in 1846 by Franciszek Maria Lanci.

363. Rozkosz Palace is situated in Ursynów district, once known as Roskosz.

364. Natolin Palace was designed by Szymon Bogumił Zug for Prince August Czartoryski, the owner of nearby Wilanów.

Monuments

365. Cobbler Jan Kiliński, a hero of the Kościuszko Insurrection, is portrayed by the 1936 monument of sculptor Stanisław Jackowski which stands in Podwale Street. He led the people of Warsaw in the uprising.

366. The column of King Sigismund III Vasa - the pride of Castle Square - is Warsaw's oldest secular monument. It commemorates the monarch who made Warsaw the capital of Poland and was founded by his son Ladislaus IV in 1644.

367. A monument to a Young Freedom-Fighter, sculpted by Jerzy Jarnuszkiewicz, adorns the Old Town walls. It commemorates the children and youths who took part in the 1944 Warsaw Uprising.

368. The Monument to the 1944 Warsaw Uprising, created by sculptor Wincenty Kućma and architect Jacek Budyn, was unveiled in Krasiński Square in 1989. It portrays freedom-fighters defending a barricade and descending into the sewers, one of whose openings is near the statue.

369. The Monument to The Fallen and Murdered in the East (Muranowska Street), the work of Maksymilian M. Biskupski, was unveiled in 1995. A railway truck full of crosses and a row of railway sleepers marked with the names of Siberian prison camps symbolise the martyrdom of Poles exiled by the Russian and Soviet authorities to Russia's remotest regions.

370. The Adam Mickiewicz Monument was unveiled in 1989 to mark the 100th anniversary of the great romantic poet's birth. The inscription on its base reads: "To the Poet from the Nation".

371. The Prince Józef Poniatowski monument stands before the Presidential Palace in Krakowskie Przedmieście. It was designed by 1817 by Danish sculptor Bertel Thorwaldsen. Tsar Nicholas I prevented its unveiling and had it transported to Russian territory. It was not until 1922, after Poland had regained its independence, that the monument was unveiled in Saski Square.

372. Andrzej Renes's monument to the Primate of the Millennium, Stefan Wyszyński, was erected in front of the Church of the Visitation Sisters.

373. The monument to Bolesław Prus, author of the novel "The Doll", was erected in 1977.

374. The Nicholas Copernicus monument was set erected in 1830 in front of Staszic Palace at the initiative of Stanisław Staszic. The author of the monument was Bertel Thorvaldsen.

375. In front of the Czapski Palace stands a statue of condotiere Bartolomeo Colleoni - a 20th-century copy of a work by Andrea Verocchia.

376. The monument of a student, sculpted by Andrzej Renes, is seated on a bench in front of the old Warsaw University Library

377. In 2001 stood in Bank Square a monument of the poet Juliusz Słowacki.

378. A monument to Stefan Starzyński, mayor of Warsaw from 1934 until Poland's capitulation in 1939, stands in Bank Square.

1945

1939

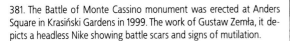

379, 380, 382. Today's Tomb of the Unknown Soldier at Piłsudski Square is all that was left of Saxon Palace, destroyed in the Second World War. In 1925, the remains of an Unknown Soldier were enshrined within the palace's arcades to commemorate the thousands of nameless Poles who died on various battle fronts fighting for Poland's freedom.

381. The Battle of Monte Cassino monument was erected at Anders Square in Krasiński Gardens in 1999. The work of Gustaw Zemła, it depicts a headless Nike showing battle scars and signs of mutilation.

383. Pawiak, a partition-era Russian tsarist prison, acquired a particularly grim reputation during the Nazi occupation. All told, some 100,000 Poles and Jews were incarcerated in the Gestapo-run prison. Its reconstructed interior now houses a museum, and a withered tree stands outside as a silent witness to history.

384. The monument to writer Maria Konopnicka was sculpted by Stanisław Kulon and erected in Saxon Gardens in 1965. It was financed through donations collected by school children.

385. In 2006, in the park outside the Palace of Culture, a monument was unveiled to Janusz Korczak, physician, educator, writer and guardian of an Orphans' Home in the Warsaw Ghetto during World War Two. Created by Zbigniew Wilma and Bohdan Chmielewski, it depicts Korczak surrounded by children against a withered tree, whose branches form a seven-candle Jewish menorah.

386. A monument to Stanisław Moniuszko, composer and author of such operas as 'Halka' and "The Haunted Manor", was unveiled in front of the Wielki Theatre in 1965. It was designed by Jan Szczepkowski.

387. In Praga district's Wileński Square stands the Brotherhood of Arms monument, popularly referred to by Warsovians as the Four Sleepers. It was erected in 1945 according to the design of Stanisław Mamot.

388. A monument to Agnieszka Osiecka, writer, poet and the author of popular song lyrics, is found in Praga's Saska Kępa quarter (Francuska Street). Sculpted by Dariusz and Teresa Kowalski, it was unveile in2007.

389. The Praga Street Orchestra Memorial (at the corner of Floriańska and Kłopotowskiego Streets), designed by Andrzej Renes, was unveiled in 2005. After sending a text message, one can hear some 100 melodies played by Praga street bands during the Nazi occupation.

390. A bridge incorporating a monument to King Jan III Sobieski, designed by Lebrun, was erected in 1788.

391. A 1909 secessionist-style monument to the outstanding Polish composer Fryderyk Chopin was unveiled in Łazienki Park in 1926. In summer, Sunday piano recitals are held at the foot of the monument.

392. The monument to the famous Polish painter Jan Matejko is found in a park in front of Szuster Palace.

393. The Józef Piłsudski monument, honouring the inter-war politician, independence activist, Marshal of Poland and creator of the Polish Legions, stands outside Belweder Palace, where he officiated as minister of war in 1926-35.

394. A Memorial to the Martyrs of Communist Terror was erected next to St Catherine's Church in Służew at a site where the victims of the communist security forces were secretly buried.

MARSZAŁEK JOZEF PIŁSUDSKI

395, 397. Saxon Gardens were laid out round the turn of the 18th century as a French-style palace park along the Saxon Axis, established by King Augustus II the Strong. The only relic surviving from that period is the garden pool, designed by Henryk Marconi. In 1727 the park was opened to the public. A 19th-century renovation transformed it into English-style gardens.

396. Ujazdów Park arose in 1893 at the intersection of the Stanislavian Axis and the Royal Way. It was laid out by Franciszek Szanior, the Warsaw's official chief gardener. The design of the bridge and pond were entrusted to William Lindley.

108

1860

398. Up until the 1944 Warsaw Uprising, Swiss Valley was Warsaw's biggest recreational park. It was established in 1825 by Polish Army Sapper Captain Stanisław Śleszyński. On a 4.5-hectare parcel of land a public park with numerous café pavilions and gazebos in the 'Swiss architecture' style was created. Its new owners expanded the park in 1855, building a Grand Avenue Salon, the city's biggest concert stage. Only a fragment of Swiss Valley has survived down to the present – a small garden with terraces and a fountain, established in 1951 at the corner of Chopin Street and Aleje Ujazdowskie.

399. Warsaw University's Botanical Gardens were laid out in 1818 at the initiative Michał Szubert and Jakub Fryderyk Hoffman.

400. A 1.5-hecatre botanical garden was been created on the roof of the Warsaw university Library.

401-402. Marshal Edward Śmigły-Rydz Park, established after the war, is one of Warsaw's youngest green areas. Its western side adjoins the Polish parliament building.

403. Traugutt Park was laid out during the inter-war period along the southern side of the Citadel's external fortifications known as Legion Fort. In the west end of the park stands the 1926 sculpture of Wacław Szymanowski entitled "Maternity".

404. As a park, the Józef Piłsudski Mokotów Meadows were created after the war, but already in the pre-war period the grassy commons served as a parade ground, a horse-racing venue and the place pioneering aerial aces Żwirko and Wigura demonstrated their skills.

405. Szczęśliwicki Park was created in the 1960s and '70s on the site of a landfill. It now hosts a year-round artificial ski slope and ski lift.

406. Praga's Ignacy Paderewski Park was established in 1906-22 by Franciszek Szanior, then director of the city's public gardens. In the post-war period until 1980, it was known as Skaryszewski Park. In the park's west end, Olga Niewska's sculpture of a 'Bathing Woman' was unveiled in 1928.

407. Stefan Żeromski Park in Żoliborz district was established in 1932 on the site of Sokolnicki's Fort, one of the Citadel's former external fortifications. Near the park's Wilson Square entrance, stands a fountain incorporating Henryk Kuna's sculpture of Alina, the girl with a jug.

408. The Polish Academy's Botanical Gardens were created in 1974 in Powsin. Plants are arranged in thematic groups including: an arboretum and collection of Polish flora as well as decorative, utility and exotic vegetation.

CEMETERS
Cemeters

409-410. Powązki Cemetery, known as Old Powązki, in Warsaw's Wola district, is the city's oldest necropolis. In 1793, the construction of St Charles Borromeo Church, designed by Dominik Merlini, was completed. Among the 2.5 million people buried there are the graves of many outstanding Poles, including writers, scientists, artists, thinkers and political figures. The cemetery A treasure trove of statuary and minor architectural works, the cemetery is under the protection of art conservators.

411-412. Powązki Military Cemetery was originally established in 1912 as a resting place for soldiers of the Russian occupation forces. In 1921, it acquired the rank of a military cemetery in which the remains of participants of the November, January, Wielkopolska and Silesian Insurrections as well as heroes of the 1920 Polish-Bolshevik War were laid to rest. Later, the fallen soldiers of the September 1939 campaign were buried there. During the communist era, it became a secular burial ground.

413. The Jewish Cemetery was established in 1806 on the outskirts of Wola. Initially, it was divided into male and female sections. At present, there are separate Orthodox, progressive, children's, orderly, military and ghetto quarters. In the Orthodox section includes a special palace where the Sacred Books are kept. Due to a lack of space, burial tak place over old graves.

414. The Tartar Muslim Cemetery (Tatarska Street) was established in 1867 after the close of the cemetery at Młynarska Street. It is the final resting place of Polish Tartars, chiefly from the lands of the Grand Duchy of Lithuania. During the Second World War, it was levelled to the ground by German tanks.

415. The Augsburg-Evangelical (Lutheran) Cemetery (ulica Młynarska Street) was established in w 1792 according to the design of the well-known Warsaw archigtect and gardener Szymon Bogumił Zuga. The Halpert Family Chapel, believed to have been designed by Antonio Corazzi, was built there in 1835. Desptie the ravages of World War Two, many relics of funereal archietcture and statuary have suirvived.

416. The Calvinist necropolis (Młynarska Street) was established together with the adjoining Augsburg-Evangelical Cemetery. during the Second World War, all the cemtery's documetnation listing who had been buried there and its buildings went up in smoke. There were many outstandu-ing Poles amongst the some 100,000 people laid to rest there.

417. Wola's eastern Orthodox Cemetery was established in reprisal for the November 1831 Insurrection. It was laid out at the site of Redoubt No. 56 of General Sowiński who defended Warsaw against the Russians. The location of a grave depended on the social rank of the deceased. The cemetery was divided into four quarters. Russian generals,

418. Warsaw Insurrectionists' Cemetery (Wolska Street 174/176) was designed by Romualda Gutt and opened in 1945 as the burial place for thousands of nameless victims whose temporary graves were scattered all over Warsaw. Some 104,000 victims of the Second World War are buried in 177 common graves. In 1973, Gustaw Zemła's monument dedicated to the 'Fallen but Undefeated' was unveiled at its entrance.

419. Wola's Karaim Cemetery (Redutowa Street 34) was established in 1890 by tobacco merchants from the Crimea. There are 40 graves in its one-hectare area. The cemetery remains open.

420. Bródno's Jewish Cemetery (Odrowąża Street) was established in 1780 by Szmul Jakubowicz Zbytkower, court banker to King Stanislaus Augustus Poniatowski. The banker also lies buried there, although in general this was a burial ground for less well-to-do members of the Jewish community.

VISTULA

421. The annals of Warsaw are closely linked to the Vistula, the greatest of Polish rivers. The first fortified castle, built at Jazdów in what is now Warsaw, stood guarded over the trading settlement of Solec where a crossing to the right-bank village of Kamion was situated. Both those settlements were already in existence in the 11th century. Over time, a dock and later a river port was later built at Solec. Barges bringing various goods from southern Poland, including salt from Wieliczka would dock there. Eventually it became necessary to join both banks of the river. That became especially important when free elections were held in the Wola meadows. Forced to precariously cross the Vistula, deputies from Małopolska and Lithuania demanded of King Sigismund Augustus that a bridge should be built. It was constructed in 1568-73, measured 500 metres and a toll was charged for crossing it. It lasted for 30 years and collapsed under the pressure of spring ice floes. The name of Ulica Mostowa (Bridge Street), which led to it, is a vestige of its existence. In 1775 at the foot of Bednarska Street, a permanent boat-mounted bridge was built and named after its investor Poniński. Toll stations were built at both ends to collect fees from travellers. The wooden bridge lasted until 1794, when it was set ablaze during the Kościuszko Insurrection to defend Warsaw against the attacking Russian forces.

422. Grot-Roweckiego Bridge, built in 1977-81, is Warsaw's biggest and widest bridge and is part of the Toruń motorway.

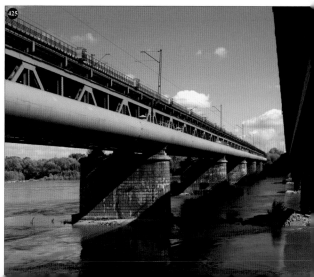

423. Warsaw's first steel bridge was the Alexandrian Bridge (named in honour of Russian Tsar Alexander), but popularly called the Kierbedź Bridge after its builder. It was originally designed as a railway bridge but during construction was adapted to road and tram traffic. Destroyed in 1944 when the East-West Thoroughfare was being built, it was replaced by a bridge designed by Silesian engineers and foundry workers from the Dąbrowa Górnicza area. In their honour, it was named the Śląsko-Dąbrowski Bridge.

424. In 1957-59, Gdańsk Bridge was built at the site of a former road and railway bridge known as the "bridge over the Citadel" which was demolished in World War Two. It is Warsaw's only twin-level bridge. A roadway for motorists is on the upper level and a tramline with pedestrian pavements – on the lower level.

425. Next to the Gdańsk Bridge is a railway bridge dating from 1921-31. Destroyed by the Germans in 1944, it was rebuilt in modified form.

426-427. The Śląsko-Dąbrowski Bridge was built in 1947-49. It replaced the former Kierbedź Bridge, Warsaw's first steel bridge built in 1859-64, which had been blown up by the Germans in 1944. Owing to its entirely new design, the Śląsko-Dąbrowski Bridge was acknowledged as a new bridge, not a re-constructed old one. It forms part of the East-West Thoroughfare which linked right-bank Praga with Warsaw's Old Town.

428, 430. The Poniatowski Bridge was built in 1904-14 after a hefty bribe persuaded Russian officials to grant permission to build it. On ther eve of an expected war with Germany, the Russians did not want to build a new crossing over the Vistula. Initially, a 700-metre viaduct constituting an extension of Aleje Jerozolimskie was built. Its neo-Renaissance architecture was designed by Stefan Szyller.

429. Suspended by 48 steel cables, Świętokrzyski Bridge, built in 1998--2000 in place of the temporary pontoon-based Mermaid Bridge, became Warsaw's first suspension bridge.

431. Two riverboats, the General Kutrzeba and the Wars, comprise Warsaw's Water Tram service which began in 2005. During the summer season, they transport passengers within Warsaw's city limits from the Citadel to Czerniaków Point.

432. "Fat Katie" is the name of a round structure anchored in the Vistula riverbed in 1964 to pump water from sub aquatic drains to the city's filtration works. That original manner of obtaining water from the riverbed is unique in the world today and is referred to as the Warsaw method.

433. Siekierkowski Bridge, built in 2000-02, is Warsaw's second suspension bridge. It is 826 metres long and forms part of the Siekierki Motorway.

434. Weeping willows are a typical element of the Masovian landscape.

435. North of Warsaw is Lake Zegrzyński, an artificial lake created in 1963 after a dam was built on the River Narew.

436. Kampinos Forest is a great forest complex situated the north-west of Warsaw. In 1959, the Kampinos National Park was created to protect many rare species of plants and wildlife.

437. The cemetery in Palmiry at the edge of Kampinos Forest contains the mass grave of more than 2,200 Warsaw inhabitants murdered there by the German Gestapo.

438. The Narrow-Gauge Railway Museum was established in Socha-czew in 1986 on the basis of a rail-line built in 1919-24 which linked the town with Wyszogród. Its collection includes more than 200 units, some 100 of which are exhibited. Every Saturday from April to September an excursion train drawn by a Diesel locomotive transports tourists over the route.

439. The Abbey of Regular Canons in Czerwińsk is situated on an escarp-ment overlooking the Vistula. The Romansque Church of the Annuncia-tion of the BVM is one of Masovia's most interesting architectural relics. Built in the latter half of the 12th century, later renovations in the Gothic, Renaissance and Baroque styles altered its appearance.

440. A romantic park was laid out in Arcadia, not far from Nieborów, in 1778 for Duchess Helena Przeździecka-Radziwiłł. It contains many struc-tures typical of that type of park, including Gothic castle ruins, Sibyl's Temple, the Arched House of the Margrave and an aqueduct.

441. Nieborów Castle was built for the Archbishop of Gniezno, Michał Stanisław Radziejowski, in 1690-96 according to Tylman of Gameren's design. French-style gardens were laid out round the palace.

442. In Łowicz, west of Warsaw, villagers don their colourful folk attire to take part in processions held on Corpus Christi.

443. Gothic Opatów Castle was built for Gniezno Archbishop Władysław Oporowski in around 1440. Renovated in the 18th and 19th centuries, it reacquired its original shape in the course of conservation efforts conducted in 1962-65, whilst retaining its Baroque elements. Built on a quadrangular foundation with an internal courtyard, it was surrounded by a moat. At present, it houses a museum of manorial period interiors.

444. The Primate's Palace in Skierniewice was built at the imitative of Wojciech Baranowski in 1609-19 in Renaissance form. It owes its present appearance to the late-Baroque renovation, conducted according to a design by Efraim Schroeger.

445. In the Classicist squire's manor house at Petrykozy the well-known actor Wojciech Siemion has established a private art gallery specialising in Polish paintings and folk art.

446. Larchwood Manor in Radziejowice was most likely built round the turn of the 19th century as the home of the steward managing the Radziejowski family grange.

447. The palace in Radziejowice owes its classicist form to the renovation carried out after 1802 by Jakub Kubicki on the structure that had stood there earlier.

448. The ruins of Czersk Castle are all that remains of the former capital of the Duchy of Masovia before it was moved to Warsaw in 1413. The castle arose at the start of the 15th century on the ruins of an earlier structure. Three round towers have survived. A draw-bridge leads to the castle.

449-450. Góra Kalwaria was established in 1666-67 to resemble Jerusalem's Mount Calvary, and royal architect Tylman of Gameren may have had a hand in the project. All that has survived of the monumental pilgrimage site are two churches and three chapels, including the Church (on the hill) of the Elevation of the Cross, built round the close of the 17th century as Pilate's Palace. The merchants' stalls dating from 1836 were designed by Bonifacy Witkowski.

451. In the Warka suburb of Winiary stands the Pułaski family's 18th-century manor house. It now houses the Kazimierz Pułaski Museum, devoted to Polish immigrants in the United States. In 1979, a monument to Kazimierz Pułaski was unveiled in front of the museum.

452. Konstancin-Jeziorna is a spa situarted south of Warsaw and popular with Warsaw residents since the late 19th century. The many splendid villas built there in the early 20th century were designed by the greatest architects of the day and reflected a variety of styles.

453. Wiązowna Palace was designed in its original Baroque form by Szymon Bogumił Zug and built for the Lubomirski family towards the end of the 18th century. In around 1890, its then owner Szymon Neumann had the palace renovated in an eclectic style including neo-Baroque elements within the buildings original walls.

454-455. The palace in Otwock Wielki was built in the late 1680s for Kazimierz Ludwik Bieliński. During the times of Grand Crown Marshal Franciszek Bieliński, after whom Warsaw's Marszałkowska Street was named, two side towers designed by royal architect Jakub Fontana were added on in 1757.

456. The Baroque church in Kobyłka from 1741-45 boast magnificent wall paintings.

457. The Milusin manor house in Sulejówek was built in 1923 by the Polish Soldier's Committee for Józef Piłsudski. It went up on a parcel of land belonging to his wife Aleksandra née Szczerbińska. In 1923-26, Marshal Piłsudski withdrew from public life to his manor house where he systematically stayed in later years as well.

458

459

458. Classicist Jabłonna Palace was built in 1774-78 for Michał Jerzy Poniatowski according to a design conceived by Dominik Merlini. Its interior was conceived by Szymon Bogumił Zug.

459. Liw Castle was built in the late 14th century and served as the seat of the dukes of Masovia. At present, it houses a collection of old weapons and a gallery of portraits from the 18th and 19th centuries.

460. The late-Baroque palace in Mińsk Mazowiecki was erected towards the end of the 17th century.

461. Modlin Fortress at the confluence of the Rivers Vistula and Narew comprises a citadel on the right bank of the Narew and two rings of forts. The first fortifications were built their during the Swedish invasion of 1655, but the bulk of the fortress was built during the Duchy of Warsaw (Napoleonic) period – 1807-12. The first major expansion of the fortress took place after the November Insurrection of 1831 had been quashed by the Russians, and one of its purposes was to prevent future Polish insurgencies.

461

460

462. The Gothic castle in Pułtusk was built for the bishops of Płock in the 15th century on the ashes of a 12th-century fortress that had been destroyed in a blaze. During the Renaissance a Great Hall was added, and during the Baroque period two characteristic towers were built onto the entrance gate. At present the structure is the seat of Polonia House.

463. The Gothic-Renaissance Basilica of the Annunciation of the BVM and St Matthew in Pułtusk was built in 1439-49 and in the 1540s. Its main nave together with the presbytery is covered with cradle vaulting.

464. The neo-Gothic palace in Opinogóra near Ciechanów was designed by Henryk Marconi and built after 1843. It was built for the outstanding poet of the Romantic period, Zygmunt Krasiński.

465. The Gothic castle of the Dukes of Masovia on the River Łyna was built in Ciechanów most likely in 1427-29 by a builder named Niklos. Subsequently elevated on two separate occasions, it was destroyed by the Swedes in 1657. In disuse from the latter half of the 18th century, it is now open to visitors as a regional museum.

466. The Gothic parish church in Ciechanów was built at the spot where St Wojciech (Adalbert) taught before setting out on his final mission journey to pagan Prussia. Relics of the Romanesque rotunda dating from that period are found beneath the presbytery.

Photography by: Stanisława, Jolanta and Rafał Jabłoński

Text: Rafał Jabłoński

Graphic design by Rafał Jabłoński

Plans: Paweł Jabłoński

Page 1: Mermaid in the Old Town Marketplace.

The photographs in this album are from the Jabłoński Family Archives.
Telephone: +48 (22) 642-06-71; cellphone: +48 602 324 409;
website: www.fotojablonski.pl,
e-mail:archiwum@fotojablonski.pl

The black and white photographs: A. Funkiewicz no: 36; S. Kris-Braun no: 27; A.
Lipka no: 25; L. Sępoliński no: 8, 11, 35, 39, 42, 58, 60, 65, 74, 77, 133, 245, 270, 283;
K. Pęcherski no: 93, 427, 430; H. Poddębski no: 46, 73, 382; St. Rossalski no: 26; W.
Szczeciński no: 34; M. Szczawik no: 37:

The photographs no 345: NCS/J.Kośnik

Print: Perfekt, Warsaw

ISBN 978-83-61511-05-2

FESTINA Publishers Warsaw
tel/fax +48 (22) 842-54-53, cellphone: +48 602 324 409
e-mail: wydawnictwo@festina.org.pl
www.festina.org.pl

WARSAW